PONS

Die drei ???®

Black Madonna

von Astrid Vollenbruch

PONS

Die drei ???®

Black Madonna

von Astrid Vollenbruch
Englisch von Marion Charles

basierend auf „Die drei ??? - Schwarze Madonna" von Astrid Vollenbruch

PONS Langenscheidt GmbH verpflichtet sich, den Zugriff auf das Hörbuch mindestens bis Ende 2026 zu gewährleisten. Einen Anspruch der Nutzung darüber hinaus gibt es nicht.

7. Auflage 2024

Übersetzung: Marion Charles
Annotationen und Übungen: Patricia Wolf
Projektmanagement: Mareike Geib
Logoentwurf: Erwin Poell, Heidelberg
Logoüberarbeitung: Sabine Redlin, Ludwigsburg
Titelillustration: Silvia Christoph, Berlin
Tonaufnahmen/Digital Mastering: allegria Musik-/Audioproduktion GbR
Sprecher: Brian Munatones
Layout/Satz: Satz und mehr, Besigheim
Druck: Multiprint Ltd., Kostinbrod

ISBN: 978-3-12-010154-3

Inhaltsverzeichnis

Inhaltsangabe

Als Peter einen verletzten jungen Mann aus dem Meer rettet, ahnt er noch nicht, dass er damit auch einen neuen Fall für die drei ??? an Land zieht. Doch schon kurze Zeit später befinden sich die drei Detektive aus Rocky Beach mitten in einem spannenden Abenteuer, in dem eine verschwundene Marienstatue die Hauptrolle spielt. Wie viele Gegner gibt es bei dieser gefährlichen Jagd? Wie weit werden sie gehen, um die begehrte Schwarze Madonna zu bekommen?

Justus, Peter und Bob stoßen an ihre Grenzen. Dieser Fall ist gefährlich, sehr gefährlich. Er bedroht sogar die Existenz ihres Detektivunternehmens...

Auftretende Personen

Justus Jonas:
Der Erste Detektiv der drei ???. Er hat ein phänomenales Gedächtnis, spricht meist in sehr gewählten Worten und trägt ein paar Pfunde zu viel mit sich herum. Justus lebt bei seinem Onkel Titus und seiner Tante Mathilda, die ein Gebrauchtwarencenter in Rocky Beach betreiben.

Peter Shaw:
Der Zweite Detektiv ist sportlich, bei Mädchen äußerst beliebt, aber manchmal etwas abergläubisch und ängstlich.

Bob Andrews:
Der Dritte Detektiv ist für Recherchen und das Archiv zuständig. Er ist ein ruhiger Zeitgenosse und sehr vernünftig.

Die Clowns:
Vier maskierte Männer, die nicht halb so lustig sind, wie sie aussehen.

José Santanda:
Ein junger mexikanischer Trödelhändler, der von den Maskierten ins Meer geworfen wird. Trotz seiner Rettung durch Peter zeigt er sich später erstaunlich unkooperativ und hat offenbar etwas zu verbergen.

Roger Pentecost:
Ein dicker, kleiner, sehr reicher Mann mit einer Schwäche für Kunstschätze, der seine Verbindungen und seinen Einfluss zu nutzen weiß. Als Inhaber der Transportfirma »Great Deliverance« organisiert er den Transport von Kunstschätzen für das Arts & Crafts Museum.

Tonio Gonzales:
Er wohnt neben José, ist abergläubisch und möchte keinen Ärger.

Fernanda Gonzales:
Tonios Frau hat deutlich mehr Mut als ihr Mann, besitzt Zivilcourage und nimmt einen weiten Weg auf sich, um etwas in Ordnung zu bringen.

Sybil Manning:
Mrs Manning ist eine sehr begabte Replikateurin, die Kunstschätze nicht nur reparieren, sondern auch ersetzen kann.

Milena Osborne:
Die Kunsthistorikerin leitet das Arts & Crafts Museum. Sie ist auf die drei ??? nicht gut zu sprechen.

1. Glitter[1] and Dust[2]

TR. 01

"Quick Bob! There's one over there!"
"At last." Bob turns on the indicator[3] and squeezes[4] his VW-Beetle into a parking space right in front of another car. The other driver shakes his fist at Bob angrily and drives off. The Three Investigators get out and stretch[5]. They have been driving up and down the Silver Canyon Road for almost an hour looking for a parking space.
For one week every year, the Carino Beach 'Glitter and Dust Festival' attracts thousands of tourists and locals. Days before dealers[6], showmen and small time artists[7] arrive in the small coastal town[8] south of Los Angeles to reserve the best places for themselves.
Justus' uncle, Titus Jonas, who manages a used car business further north[9] in Rocky Beach also sets up his stand here for a few days. And the Three Investigators have promised[10] to help him with sales at the weekend.
They grab[11] their bags and start walking. It isn't a pleasure to walk on asphalt in the heat of the Californian summer and all three are soaked in sweat[12] when they finally reach[13] Carino Beach.

1 glitter: Glitzer
2 dust: Staub
3 indicator: Blinker
4 to squeeze: quetschen
5 to stretch: sich strecken, dehnen
6 dealer: Händler
7 small time artists: Kleinkünstler
8 coastal town: Küstenstadt
9 further north: weiter nördlich
10 to promise: versprechen
11 to grab: greifen, grabschen
12 soaked in sweat: schweißüberströmt
13 to reach: erreichen

Already, quite a lot is going on[1]. Market stalls are lined up on the right and left. The owners are unpacking their goods[2].
All around, there are food stalls with food from all over the world. The multinational city, Los Angeles, is represented by all shades of skin[3], ages and all classes. Policemen are patrolling the streets to keep fights and theft[4] under control. Carino Beach pier looks like a bridge[5] which reaches into the sea and ends abruptly after about 100 yards[6]. The pier serves[7] as a further base[8] for traders.
"Our stand is over there," Justus calls out. "Uncle Titus actually managed[9] to get a spot on the pier."
"Couldn't he have built it up in the water?"
Peter looks longingly[10] at the huge waves breaking on the beach shore[11].
"Blast[12]! Why didn't I bring my surfboard!"
Justus begins, "Well, because we promised to ..."
"... help your uncle. Yes, yes. I know."
As they empty[13] their water bottles, Justus brings them all ice cream. He has almost caught up[14] with Peter and Bob when someone pushes him aside. Justus stumbles[15], loses his balance, and drops the ice cream.

1 sth is going on: es ist etwas los
2 goods: Waren
3 shades of skin: (Schattierungen der) Hautfarben
4 theft: Diebstahl
5 bridge: Brücke
6 yard: *Längenmaß, entspricht 91,44 cm*
7 to serve: dienen
8 a further base: eine weitere Plattform
9 actually managed: tatsächlich geschafft
10 longingly: sehnsüchtig
11 huge waves breaking on the beach shore: riesige Wellen, die sich an der Sandküste brechen
12 blast (*Umgangssprache*): verdammt, Mist
13 to empty: ausleeren
14 to catch up with sb: jemanden einholen
15 to stumble: stolpern

"Watch out!" he calls out angrily.
The man who pushed him turns around briefly. Justus stops instinctively. From behind, the guy[1] looks quite normal – dark hair, light shirt, jeans, tanned[2] and strong. But he is wearing a white plastic clown mask with a red nose over his face. His broad, staring grin[3] would look funny in a circus ring, but here it seems quite out of place.
"You pushed me over," Justus calls out. "Now you can pay me for the ice cream!"
The man stares coldly at Justus; then he turns around without a word and walks on. Three other men are following[4] him. Two are equally[5] big and strong, but one is a little smaller and thinner[6]. All three are wearing clown masks with ordinary[7] T-shirts and jeans.
"Wait!" Justus calls after them, but they ignore him.
Like bulldozers, they push their way through the crowd and anyone who doesn't get out of the way fast enough is pushed aside roughly[8], just like Justus. Peter and Bob now reach the First Investigator.
The ice cream melts[9] into an unappetizing sticky sauce[10] in the hot sand.
"What a mess[11]!" Peter complains[12]. "Oh well, let's go and get some new ice cream."
They line up again at the ice cream van.

1 guy (*Umgangssprache*): Typ, Kerl
2 tanned: braungebrannt
3 broad, staring grin: breites Grinsen und Starren
4 to follow: folgen
5 equally: gleich, ebenso
6 thin: dünn
7 ordinary: gewöhnlich, normal
8 roughly: rau
9 to melt: schmelzen
10 unappetizing sticky sauce: unappetitliche klebrige Soße
11 mess: Durcheinander
12 to complain: sich beschweren

"Who were those guys?" Justus throws a look in the direction in which the four men disappeared[1].
"One thing is for sure, they were not funny clowns."
"Is our criminal intelligence required[2] again?" Peter teases[3]. "Can't we ever have a day's holiday away from being investigators? Just like everybody else?"
"I'd like to know."
"They probably belong to a fairground[4] and simply haven't taken off their costumes."
They get their ice cream, Bob pays and then they make their way to Uncle Titus' junk store[5] on the pier. First, they help to sort out the junk and set up the store. So far[6], no costumed people are in sight, only tradesmen[7] strolling[8] around among the stores.
Slowly the sun sinks into the ocean. The tide[9] comes in and the beach umbrellas and chairs are taken in. On the pier, the first lamps are switched on. The Three Investigators are just settling down[10] in their sleeping bags among the heaps[11] of junk, when suddenly there is a loud noise near them. There is an argument[12] in one of the stalls. Four men are attacking a trader, a young Mexican, who shrinks back[13] into the railing.
"It's those clowns from earlier," Peter shouts.

1 to disappear: verschwinden
2 required: notwendig, erforderlich
3 to tease: hänseln, necken
4 fairground: Jahrmarkt
5 junk store: Schrottwarenladen
6 so far: bisher
7 tradesmen: Händler
8 to stroll: spazieren, flanieren
9 tide: Flut
10 to settle down: sich niederlassen
11 heap: großer Haufen
12 argument: Auseinandersetzung
13 to shrink back: zurückschrecken, ausweichen

The Three Investigators jump up. Other traders notice them, too. But before anyone can do anything, two of the masked men tip the trader's table over. The Mexican screams and tries to hold on to his table, but the other two men hold him back. The table falls over, crashes against the railing and all the junk slips off. Some pieces crash on to the pier and break. But the rest falls into the water five yards below. The masked men double up with laughter[1] – then the tallest of the men takes hold of the trader and lifts him up effortlessly[2].
"You are attached to your stuff[3], right? Then go and get it!"
And he flings him over the railing.
With a cry, the young man falls and disappears into the ocean.
Justus, Peter and Bob, who were watching the scene, are shocked and run over to the railing. Down below a few puzzles, games and figurines are tossing[4] about in the water. The waves hit the pier's pillars[5]. The young man has disappeared. And he doesn't emerge[6] again.

Detective Question

Why can't the Three Investigators once again enjoy their holidays in peace?

1 to double up with laughter: platzen vor Lachen
2 effortlessly: mühelos
3 you are attached to your stuff (*Umgangssprache*): du hängst an deinem Zeug
4 to toss: werfen, schleudern
5 pillar: Pfeiler
6 to emerge: auftauchen, erscheinen

2. The Hero[1] of Carino Beach

TR. 02

The next minute, the four men disappear. Peter climbs onto the railing and jumps. With a splash[2] he dives[3] into the water which, after the heat of the pier, seems icy cold.

Although the ocean is only five metres deep and really quite warm, the shock takes his breath[4] away. He opens his eyes and looks around in the dim[5] water. The young man is nowhere to be seen. Peter emerges. Someone throws a life belt[6] to him. He holds onto it and looks around. Over there he can see some movement!

Peter peers[7] through the water and sees a figure disappear in the shadows under the pier.

He grabs the life belt and pulls it along behind him as he swims towards the pillars. The waves keep on throwing him back, only at the last moment he notices a huge jagged splinter[8] sticking out[9] of the wood.

Peter looks for a different place, throws the life belt up on the pillar and climbs up behind it. Then he sees the young trader who is dripping wet and crouching[10] in-between the pillars.

His T-shirt and shorts are sticking to his body, he is shaking violently[11] and is pressing one hand to his chest[12]. The coloured T-shirt is torn and

1 hero: Held
2 splash: Platscher, Aufspritzen
3 to dive: tauchen
4 breath: Atem
5 dim: trüb
6 life belt: Rettungsring
7 peer: spähen
8 jagged splinter: gezackter Splitter
9 to stick out: herausragen
10 to crouch: kauern, hocken
11 violently: heftig
12 chest: Brustkorb

soaked[1] through with blood. He must have injured[2] himself on the splinter[3] when he climbed out of the water.
Peter carefully climbs over to the injured man. Now he can see that the Mexican is only a few years older than he is. The young man's face is distorted by pain[4].
"Did Shef send you after me?" he groans. "Go away, leave me alone!"
"What did you say?" Peter asks puzzled. "What Jeff? No, nobody sent me! And with an injury like that you belong in a hospital. What's your name?"
"José Santanda. But I –"
"I'm Peter Shaw. Give me your hand, I'll help you."
Peter sounds more confident[5] than he is because he has no idea how to get José onto the beach. The Mexican shakes his head and refuses[6] to take Peter's hand. Suddenly, however, he grows pale[7], his eyes roll back and he topples over[8]. Peter only just catches him before he slides into the water. Peter looks around in despair[9]. He hears the excited voices of the traders on the pier above his head.
"Hello!" he shouts. But no one can hear him because of the roaring[10] waves.
Suddenly a bright light pierces[11] his eyes. Blinded, he squeezes them shut and hears the humming[12] of a motor. A boat! He waves wildly and shouts: "Here!"

1 soaked: durchnässt
2 injured: verletzt
3 splinter: Splitter, Spreißel, Holzspan
4 distorted by pain: schmerzverzerrt
5 confident: zuversichtlich
6 to refuse: verweigern
7 pale: blass
8 to topple over: umfallen
9 despair: Verzweiflung
10 roaring: rauschend
11 to pierce: stechen, blenden
12 humming: Brummen

A moment later the boat is there. José doesn't wake up as two men and Peter heave[1] him into the boat, but as soon as he is lying on the wooden floor, he reaches for Peter's hand. Peter bends down to understand what José is saying above the noise of the engine.
"The Black Madonna," José murmurs[2]. "They want to know where she is. Don't tell them!"
"What Black Madonna?" Peter asks, surprised.
"Forty six Laguna Street! A statue! Under my bed! Bring her –"
The engine shudders[3] and dies. The boat is grounded on the beach where the ambulance, surrounded by curious onlookers[4], is waiting with blinking lights.
Peter quickly bends down to José again. "Where shall I bring her?" But he is already pushed aside roughly.
"Get away, boy!"
Two men in white clothing lift José out of the boat onto the stretcher[5] and carry him into the ambulance. The door closes, the men get in. With sirens blaring[6], the ambulance pushes through the crowd, drives along the street and disappears.
Peter stands there a little lost until a flashlight suddenly blinds him. A thin blond man in jeans and a yellow T-shirt with a digital camera in his hand is standing in front of him.
"Hello young man! What's your name?"
"Peter Shaw," Peter stutters,[7] caught unawares[8].
"Peter Shaw, aha! So, Peter, how do you feel being a life saver? Do you come from Carino Beach?"
"No, from Rocky Beach."

1 to heave: stemmen, hieven
2 to murmur: murmeln
3 to shudder: zittern, stottern
4 onlookers: Zuschauer, Schaulustige
5 stretcher: Trage, Tragbahre
6 sirens blaring: heulende Sirene
7 to stutter: stottern
8 unawares: überrascht

Peter doesn't know what to say. "I only –"
But then Justus turns up, briskly[1] pushes the man aside and stands in front of Peter. Loudly, he says: "My colleague[2] doesn't give interviews and if anyone photographs him without permission, they will hear from his lawyer[3]. Good evening!"
"Listen, boy! You can't do that!" the reporter objects. "There is a public interest in –"
"Which paper do you work for?"
"That's none of your business."
"Then you're out of luck. All exclusive rights for this story have already been sold to the Los Angeles Post. Terribly sorry. Good bye!"
"Who are you by the way? Why are you poking[4] your nose where it doesn't belong?"
"And who are you? Can I please see your ID card[5]?"
The man puts his camera into his bag, and when he looks up again his eyes have narrowed[6]. The gaunt[7] face has taken on a severe[8] expression. "I'm somebody who can make a whole lot of trouble for you and your friend. Nobody quarrels[9] with me."
He turns around and leaves.
"Come on, Peter!" hisses[10] Bob, who has crept up to Peter unnoticed.
Peter follows him, relieved. He feels very cold in his wet clothes and is trembling[11]. Justus follows his friend slowly, deep in thought.

1 briskly: energisch, lebhaft
2 colleague: Kollege
3 lawyer: Anwalt
4 to poke one's nose in: sich einmischen, seine Nase hineinstecken
5 ID card: Ausweis
6 narrowed eyes: schmale Augen
7 gaunt: hager
8 severe: ernst
9 to quarrel: streiten, sich anlegen mit
10 to hiss: zischen
11 to tremble: zittern

Peter changes[1] on the beach. Meanwhile, Uncle Titus has come back and wants to know what happened.
"That was an odd[2] reporter, don't you think?" Justus says.
Bob, a reporter's son, just grins.
"All reporters are odd. What exactly do you mean?"
"First of all, I think it's strange that he appeared so quickly."
"I don't find that strange at all. All newspapers in the area are going to report about the festival and naturally they send a reporter. The guy just happened to be nearby."
"Secondly, the reporter didn't want to tell me which paper he works for!"
"That really is unusual," Bob agrees. "And thirdly?"
"Thirdly. What kind of reporter threatens[3] an unwilling interviewee[4]?"
"Hm. Surely, you have a theory already."
"I have," said Justus. "I don't think this guy was a reporter. One of the clowns was a little smaller and thinner, and he could have been this man. And when Peter jumped into the water, he wanted to find out who was interfering."
"I don't like it, boys," says Uncle Titus. "You shouldn't quarrel with people like that. Luckily, he doesn't know who you are ... or ..."
"Yes," says Peter and bites his lip[5].
"When he was there all of a sudden asking questions, I told him my name. And also that I come from Rocky Beach. Sorry, Justus ... I'm an idiot!"
"You couldn't know. On the other hand, it's annoying[6]. Oh well, it's over. I don't think we'll ever hear from him again."

1 to change: sich umziehen
2 odd: seltsam, eigenartig
3 to threaten: bedrohen
4 unwilling interviewee: unwilliger Informant
5 to bite one's lips: sich auf die Lippen beißen
6 annoying: ärgerlich

"Perhaps we will," Peter sighs[1]. "I've got to tell you something: I think we have a new case."

3 Half an hour later, they are sitting in Bob's car and drive around the streets of Carino Beach.
"So," says Justus. "This José Santanda believes that the clowns are after the Black Madonna and they want to find out from him where she is. He isn't telling them and so they wreck[2] his stall and throw him into the water. José asks you if someone called Jeff has sent you – perhaps that is our fake[3] reporter. And before he loses consciousness,[4] he asks you to fetch the statue from its hiding place and to bring it to a place or a person, who or where he can't tell you before he passes out[5]."
"That's right," says Peter. "And it sounds as if it was very important to him that the statue of the Madonna was brought there, wherever that is."
"Good, then we have to find out who she is supposed[6] to be for and deliver her there. Perhaps we can find a clue[7] in this flat[8]."
Laguna Street is a neglected[9] and shabby street[10] in the east part of the town. Nearly all the houses are smeared with graffiti[11]. All shutters[12] are secured by padlocks[13]. There is no one about, but now and then

1 to sigh: seufzen
2 to wreck: demolieren, zerstören
3 fake: falsch
4 to lose consciousness: das Bewusstsein verlieren
5 to pass out: bewusstlos werden
6 to be supposed to be for: bestimmt sein für
7 to find a clue: einen Hinweis finden
8 flat: Wohnung
9 neglected: schäbig, vernachlässigt
10 shabby street: heruntergekommene Straße
11 smeared with graffiti: mit Graffiti beschmiert
12 shutters: Fensterläden
13 padlock: Vorhängeschloss

they hear scraps of music and children's cries through the windows of the upper stories[1].

House number 46 is no different from the others. It has a gray front with locked shutters that are covered with graffiti. The front door is made out of wood and has no handle, only a keyhole[2]. Justus tries all four bells[3], but the door remains closed.

Justus glances[4] at Peter, "Do you have your skeleton key[5] with you, Second Investigator?"

"Yes, I think so, but I don't think we should do that."

"Why not? It's an emergency after all. José himself begged[6] you to fetch the Madonna from his flat."

Peter hesitates[7], shrugs[8] his shoulders and pulls out the skeleton key from his bag. He pokes the lock with it until it springs open. The Three Investigators go in and Bob switches on the flashlight which he brought along just in case.

The beam of light shines onto a stack of boxes, empty bottles and rubbish bags. Two doors lead off the corridor on the right, and on the left, the stairway leads upstairs. Bob lights up the two doors and looks at Justus. The First Investigator nods[9]. Soundlessly, they creep[10] to the first door, but somebody called Gonzales lives there. They have more luck with the second door.

"J.S.," whispers Justus. "José Santanda. Pass the skeleton key, Second Investigator."

"Wait," Bob hisses. "We don't need that. The door is open."

1 upper stories: obere Stockwerke
2 keyhole: Schlüsselloch
3 bell: Klingel
4 to glance at: anschauen, einen Blick werfen auf
5 skeleton key: Dietrich, Multifunktionsschlüssel
6 to beg: bitten
7 to hesitate: zögern
8 to shrug: mit den Achseln zucken
9 to nod: nicken
10 to creep: schleichen

All three stop dead[1], but nothing moves behind the door. Justus gives the door a careful push and it opens with a creak[2]. The flashlight lights up the apartment. For a moment, they stand there as if paralyzed[3]. Then Bob says hoarsely[4], "I think the clowns were quicker than we were!"

Detective Question

Why do you think the clowns were quicker than the Three Investigators?

1 to stop dead: erstarren
2 creak: Knarren
3 paralyzed: gelähmt
4 hoarsely: heiser

3. Burglary with Consequences TR. 04

The apartment has been completely ransacked[1]. There is an overturned[2] small shoe cupboard[3] in the corridor. The coat hooks[4] are torn out of the wall. And as the Three Investigators creep stealthily[5] into the flat, pieces of mirror crunch under their shoes.

"Quiet," Peter whispers.

In the light[6], they are confronted by an ugly scene. Someone has tried to destroy[7] the whole flat. All cupboards are torn open, the drawers[8] smashed and their contents thrown onto the floor. The cushions[9] on the sofa are slit open[10], the books pulled off their shelves and the shelves are knocked over.

"Give me the flashlight," Justus whispers to Bob and creeps towards the door, which is hanging from only one hinge[11].

A board creaks under his feet and all three freeze. But nothing moves. Somewhere in the apartment house, the sound of a television drones[12] on.

Justus creeps on and opens the door. Behind it is a simply furnished[13] bedroom. Here too, the burglars have destroyed as much as possible. Justus shines the light under the bed. An object about an arm's length

1 ransacked: durchwühlt
2 overturned: umgestürzt
3 shoe cupboard: Schuhschrank
4 coat hooks: Garderobenhaken
5 to creep stealthily: verstohlen anschleichen
6 in the light: bei Licht
7 to destroy: zerstören
8 drawer: Schublade
9 cushion: Kissen
10 slit open: aufgeschlitzt
11 hinge: Türangel, Scharnier
12 to drone: dröhnen
13 simply furnished: einfach eingerichtet

had lain[1] there. Now only a blurred imprint[2] is left in the dust. A sharp, unpleasant smell lingers in the air.
Justus straightens up and goes back into the wrecked living room. "Well, mates, the Black Madonna is gone."
"Are you sure?" asks Bob. "Perhaps she's in the kitchen."
He tiptoes[3] a few steps forward and shines the flashlight into the kitchen.
"Look out!" Peter shouts.
Four figures charge out of the kitchen straight towards Bob, who is completely taken by surprise. For a moment, the clowns' garish[4] masks light up, then one of the men pushes him aside. Bob trips over a ragged[5] sofa cushion and falls. The next minute, the burglars run outside. The front door slams[6] shut.
"Follow them!" Justus shouts.
The Three Investigators come out of the flat, past a man who is peeping[7] out of the neighboring[8] door. He yells[9] Spanish curses[10] at them as they run out of the house.
"Over there!" Justus calls and points down the street where the four figures are running around the corner.
"Bob, quick!"
A few seconds later, they are sitting in Bob's VW-Beetle and slam the doors. Bob turns on the engine and the Beetle takes off. Unfortunately, the Beetle doesn't move quickly, but rather bumpily[11] and

1 had lain: hatte gelegen
2 blurred imprint: verwischte Spur
3 to tiptoe: auf Zehenspitzen gehen
4 garish: grell
5 ragged: zerfetzt
6 to slam shut: zuschlagen
7 to peep: (verstohlen) schauen
8 neighboring: benachbart
9 to yell: rufen, schreien
10 curse: Fluch
11 bumpily: holprig

slowly. Bob accelerates[1], but it is no good. When they turn around the corner, the street is already completely empty.

"That was successful from start to finish," Bob says as he drives back to the beach.
"Right," Justus agrees. "But now we know that there's a third party in this game."
"How do you come to that conclusion?"
"No one carried anything that looked like a statue. So they didn't find anything and arrived too late, just as we did. Someone else has already taken the Madonna."
"Perhaps they left it in the kitchen," says Peter.
"Why should they do that?"
"Because we arrived before they could get away."
"Peter, they were four grown[2] men! However brilliant[3] we may be – we can't compete[4] with that. They could have carried out the statue, as well as half the contents of the flat without us being able to stop them."
Justus grows silent and bites his lower lip.
Bob throws him a glance[5]. "What are you thinking about?"
"There was something ... an unpleasant chemical smell which didn't fit into the flat. I wonder what that was."
With a gloomy[6] expression, he listens to the fast approaching[7] wailing[8] of a siren[9].

1 to accelerate: beschleunigen, Gas geben
2 grown: erwachsen
3 brilliant: brilliant, genial
4 to compete with: dagegen ankommen, damit konkurrieren
5 to throw sb a glance: jemandem einen Blick zuwerfen
6 gloomy: düster
7 to approach: näher kommen
8 wailing: Geheul
9 siren: Sirene

"Obviously, the neighbor has already called the police. We can't go back and look around the flat anymore."

5 It is late when they get back to the pier. Uncle Titus tells them that they have to drive back to Rocky Beach the next day. While they were away, he had an argument with the organizer who called the attack on José a "private matter" between Mexicans, despite[1] all the witnesses[2] saying that the attackers had been white. He doesn't want to do anything about it and as Uncle Titus doesn't like this way of thinking, he decides to leave 'Glitter and Dust' for the time being. The next morning, at 5:30 a.m., they pack everything up with the help of a few assistants and start off home.
On the way over the pier, the Three Investigators take the opportunity to ask the traders about the clowns, but don't get much of a result. Everyone saw the gang, but nobody noticed anything except the masks. At least a furniture[3] salesman remembers that one of the three had a light crew cut[4].

"I'll never rescue[5] anyone again." With these words, Peter tears open[6] the door of the headquarters on Sunday. Justus and Bob wince[7].
"OK, Peter," says Justus. "What's the matter?"
"What's the matter? Oh nothing! Except that my mother went mad all day about the fact that I'd thrown myself into the ocean among the sharks[8] only to get into the newspaper's headlines. And every time I convince her that it wasn't like that, a reporter rings the bell to talk to the hero of Carino Beach! I've had enough!"

1 despite: trotz
2 witness: Zeuge
3 furniture: Möbel
4 crew cut: Bürstenschnitt, Kurzhaarschnitt
5 to rescue: retten
6 to tear open: aufreißen
7 to wince: zusammenzucken
8 sharks: Haie

"Did the fake reporter turn up, too?" Bob asks curiously.
"Luckily no."
"By the way, Inspector Cotta is expecting us," says Justus. "Carino Beach is not under his jurisdiction[1], but he wants to question us about a burglary on Laguna Street."
"What?" Peter is aghast[2].
"How does he know – I mean, why does he believe that we know something about it?"
"He didn't want to tell." says Justus. "It really isn't Cotta's district, but while we drive there you can tell us what you found out about the Black Madonna, Bob."
"So," Bob says five minutes later in the car. "I've only done research[3] on the internet. 'Madonna' is Italian for 'my lady' and refers to Mary, mother of God. There are places of worship[4] in Europe where they say that she appeared. Thousands of people go on pilgrimage[5] in order to pray[6] to her statue and ask her for help. Apparently, miracles[7] often happen there – invalids are healed and so on. Many of these statues are made of light wood or are brightly colored[8], but there are also quite a few black Madonnas. They are also found in Turkey and Russia, and even in India. Some were black from the beginning, either because they were made of black wood or because they were painted black, others were blackened later. There are also some pictures – the best known one is the Black Madonna of Tschenstochau, a painting which became almost completely black from candle smoke[9] in the

1 jurisdiction: Zuständigkeit, Gerichtsbarkeit
2 aghast: entsetzt
3 research: Forschung
4 worship: Anbetung, Verehrung
5 pilgrimage: Pilgerreise
6 to pray: beten
7 miracle: Wunder
8 brightly colored: in bunten Farben
9 candle smoke: Kerzenruß

course of past centuries[1]. Then I looked for the Madonna here in California. There is a Madonna guest house, a Madonna road, a Mount Madonna Sanitarium, and the singer Madonna. And seven years ago, a Madonna was stolen from the Museum of Arts and Crafts[2]. None of these Madonnas are black."

Bob stops his story and drives into the parking lot in front of the police headquarters. They get out, show their IDs[3] at the entrance and are immediately lead into Inspector Cotta's office.

"Good morning, Inspector," Justus begins.

"Morning, Justus," Inspector Cotta replies angrily. "Hello, Peter and Bob. Tell me, what have you got yourselves into this time!"

"Why, what's up?" asks Peter.

"Oh, haven't you read today's Sunday edition[4] of the Carino Daily Post yet? Then it's high time!"

He pulls a newspaper out of a drawer and throws it onto the table.

"Sit down and make yourselves comfortable[5] and I'll fetch myself a cup of coffee, while I decide which cell I should reserve for you."

Justus, Peter and Bob exchange alarmed looks[6] and then look at the paper. The article in the back is marked by a thick red felt pen, "Heroic[7] rescue or nasty deceit[8]?"

With the two headlines, "Investigator Trio gone astray[9]" and "After lifesaving[10], they break in[11]," the article goes on in detail about the dramatic rescue of an injured man by a well known youth investigator trio, then goes on, "worried neighbor calls the police." And then

1 century: Jahrhundert
2 Museum of Arts & Crafts: Museum für Kunsthandwerk
3 ID (identity card): Ausweis
4 Sunday edition: Sonntagsausgabe
5 to make onself comfortable: es sich bequem/gemütlich machen
6 to exchange alarmed looks: erschrockene Blicke wechseln
7 heroic: heldenhaft
8 nasty deceit: gemeiner Betrug
9 to go astray: sich auf Abwegen befinden
10 lifesaving: Lebensrettung
11 to break in: einbrechen

makes the assumption[1] that Peter stole José's front door key during the rescue so he could rob[2] his flat later, while the victim[3] was still "fighting for his life." The article was written by someone called B.S.

While they are reading the report, Inspector Cotta comes back with his cup of coffee and a little box, sits down and waits until they are finished. Then he says: "Well?"

Detective Question

Why are the Three Investigators in trouble now?

1 assumption: Vermutung
2 to rob: ausrauben
3 victim: Opfer

4. Under Suspicion[1]

TR. 06

Justus' brain is working at full speed. "There's really something wrong with this story," he says. "Is the article only in the Carino Daily Post? Or in other papers too?"

"The others praised[2] Peter for his heroic deed[3]," says Cotta. "That's okay. Is it true what the paper says? Of course, you don't have to answer if that incriminates[4] you."

Bob looks up. "Do you really believe we would steal someone's key and then enter their apartment and wreck[5] everything?"

"What I believe isn't important," Cotta mutters[6]. Then he looks at the Three Investigators one by one and shakes his head. "But in case it makes you feel better, no, I don't believe it."

He leans back and crosses his arms. "So tell me what you did to get the Carino Daily Post to come after you?"

"I believe, we annoyed a reporter because we refused[7] to let him have a story," Justus says.

"He got it all the same," says Cotta. "What with[8] the break-in immediately after the rescue, you gave him enough material. What happened?"

Justus briefly tells him how they found the flat and how they were interrupted by the four men.

"Ah," Inspector Cotta comments. "I have a statement[9] here from a Mr. Tonio Gonzales. He says he heard suspicious[10] sounds coming from

1 suspicion: Verdacht
2 to praise: loben
3 deed: Tat
4 to incriminate: belasten
5 wreck: zerstören
6 to mutter: murmeln
7 to refuse: verweigern
8 what with (*Redewendung*): wegen
9 statement: Zeugenaussage
10 suspicious: verdächtig

the neighboring flat and when he went to check, he saw three – not four – flee to the exit. The description of these three young men fits you surprisingly[1] well – one rather overweight[2] person, one small one with glasses and a tall, burly[3] one."

"That's interesting," Justus observes. "Mr. Gonzales didn't see the four men who ran out beforehand[4]?"

"Obviously not, otherwise he would have mentioned[5] them."

"Amazing," says Justus.

"He might have recognized Peter and me, but definitely not Bob – certainly not last night, because Bob wasn't wearing his glasses. He was wearing contact lenses[6], just as he is now," he goes on while Inspector Cotta and Peter are looking at Bob, dumbfounded[7]. "I wonder where he got our description[8] from. And what does he gain[9] from causing us problems by giving a false statement?"

The Inspector makes a note. "We'll ask him about this again. You're right, Justus, something doesn't seem right here. But that doesn't alter the fact that you broke into a flat."

"With permission of the owner," Peter now says. "Why don't you ask José?"

"I'd like to do that but it's not possible. José Santanda collapsed[10] last night and is still in a coma[11]. Obviously he was fairly[12] ill beforehand and the injury made him worse. We're looking for his family, but until now

1 surprisingly: überraschend
2 overweight: übergewichtig
3 burly: kräftig, stämmig
4 beforehand: vorher
5 to mention: erwähnen
6 contact lenses: Kontaktlinsen
7 dumbfounded: verblüfft
8 description: Beschreibung
9 to gain: gewinnen, etwas davon haben
10 to collapse: Kollaps erleiden
11 coma: Koma
12 fairly: ziemlich

we have only found his previous employer[1], a Mr. Pentecost. He's the owner of a logistics company. José worked for him as a driver until half a year ago. Mr. Pentecost was horrified[2] when he heard about José's accident. And he offered to employ him again as soon as he recovers[3]."

"Why was José fired[4]?" Bob asks.

"The company didn't have enough orders[5]."

"Thank you very much," says Justus. "Then we'll visit Mr. Pentecost and question him –"

"Oh no, Justus Jonas," says Inspector Cotta. "You won't do anything like that. You go home and wait until the young Mr. Santanda wakes up and exonerates[6] you."

He opens a small box which he had brought with him. It contains a finger printing set. "Hold out your fingers, I have to compare your fingerprints[7] with those in the flat."

"And now?" asks Bob, back in the car again.

"We'll visit the Carino Daily Post," Justus decides. "It could be that B.S. is a normal reporter who only wants to get revenge[8] on us because we spoiled[9] his story. But then he's surprisingly well informed – how did he know that we were in Laguna Street? And if he's one of the clowns who wants to cast suspicion on us, we should take a closer look at him."

1 previous employer: vorheriger Arbeitgeber
2 horrified: entsetzt
3 to recover: sich erholen
4 to fire: kündigen, entlassen
5 order: Bestellung
6 to exonerate: entlasten
7 fingerprint: Fingerabdruck
8 revenge: Rache
9 to spoil: verderben

"I don't know," Peter says doubtfully[1]. "Perhaps B.S. also happened to be in Laguna Street when the break-in took place."
"I don't believe in coincidences[2], especially when B.S. is trying to make us look guilty. And José's neighbor clearly didn't recognize us. I believe that someone doesn't like us and that someone told Gonzales who he should recognize[3] and who not."
"Perhaps B.S. himself?" Bob says. "He doesn't like us for sure. But to convince[4] Gonzales he would have had to be on the scene before the police."
"Then he would only have just missed us," says Peter. "Perhaps he saw us and gave Gonzales the description."
Justus shakes his head. "Then he wouldn't have made the mistake of mentioning the glasses."
It is already afternoon when, after an exhausting[5] ride in the scorching heat[6], they arrive in the industrial area of the small coastal town and go into the Carino Daily Post building. But they are unlucky there. The gate keeper sitting behind the counter[7] claims[8] that he doesn't know anybody with the initials B.S. Perhaps a freelancer[9], but no one on staff.
"Fine." Justus takes out a business card, writes his telephone number on it and puts it on the counter.
"In case he does come by, please give this to him."
The man reads the business card and raises his eyebrows.

1 doubtfully: zweifelnd
2 coincidence: Zufall
3 to recognize: wiedererkennen
4 to convince: überzeugen
5 exhausting: anstrengend
6 scorching heat: sengende Hitze
7 counter: Rezeption, Theke
8 to claim: behaupten
9 freelancer: Freischaffender, freier Mitarbeiter

"Wait a minute. Are you the rascals[1] from the pier and the burglary?"
Now Justus has enough.
"We are honorary police assistants from Rocky Beach. And you can tell Mr. B.S. that we won't put up with such behavior[2]. Either[3] he makes it clear in his next article that there isn't any proof[4] that we broke in somewhere or we will sue him for libel[5]. Have a nice day!"

Detective Question

Is the devious reporter really seeking revenge because the Three Investigators spoiled his story?

1 rascal: Bengel, Gauner
2 behavior: Verhalten
3 either … or: entweder … oder
4 proof: Beweis/e
5 libel: Verleumdung

5. A Visit to the Museum

TR. 07

On the way home, they get stuck[1] in a traffic jam. Bob has the brilliant idea of driving along Wilshire Boulevard, not only home of Los Angeles' most important museums, but also of several parks, entertainment centres and financial buildings. A thick layer of exhaust fumes[2] envelope the unending line of cars in grey smog.
Justus sniffs[3].
"Don't breathe," Bob warns.
"The smell reminds me of something, but I'm not sure what." He frowns[4] and sniffs again.
Justus sits up.
"What do you think about a visit to a museum?"
Bob catches on[5] at once. "Because of the stolen Madonna? But that was seven years ago, Justus!"
"Doesn't matter, just as long as we get off this road."

The Arts and Crafts Museum is in a large park with other buildings next to the Wilshire Boulevard. Here, too, the air smells of smog and gasoline[6], but the park seems out of place in this modern city with its millions of people, skyscrapers[7], glitzy[8] film industry and traffic jams. The park itself is an excavation site[9] where the remains of mammoths[10], razor-toothed tigers[11] and other kinds of animals which lived in this

1 to get stuck in a traffic jam: im Stau stehen
2 exhaust fumes: Abgase
3 to sniff: schnuppern
4 to frown: die Stirn runzeln
5 to catch on: etwas kapieren
6 gasoline: Benzin
7 skyscraper: Wolkenkratzer
8 glitzy: glitzernd
9 excavation site: Ausgrabungsort
10 mammoth: Mammut
11 razor-toothed tiger: Säbelzahntiger

area over 15,000 years ago have been found. These findings are on display in the George C. Page museum, next to the Arts and Crafts Museum. A group of three mammoths is standing next to the street. A fourth young mammoth is tied onto the loading area[1] of a truck[2]. The animal's trunk[3] has been broken off and its head and back are smeared[4] with graffiti.
The Three Investigators get out of the VW-Beetle.
A young man comes out of the museum, climbs into the truck's cab[5] and drives off with the mammoth; obviously to have it repaired and cleaned. They go into the Arts and Crafts Museum where there is an exhibition of Italian Renaissance art. The first thing they see is a statue of the Madonna, nearly nine foot[6] tall, gleaming[7] white. She seems to welcome them, smiling, arms spread out[8]. There are even more statues of the Mother of God in different sizes standing in recesses[9]. Paintings of Italian towns and sceneries from the 16th century are hanging on the walls.
"Odd," says Bob and turns the pages of his museum guide[10], which he bought at the entrance[11]. "It says here that it was a Madonna with a goblet[12] that was stolen seven years ago. But she's standing over there!"
He points to a small recess in which there is a colored figure, three foot tall. The Three Investigators go to the recess and look at the statue in detail.

1 loading area: Ladefläche
2 truck: LKW
3 trunk: Rüssel
4 smeared: beschmiert
5 the truck's cab: Führerhaus des LKW
6 foot: *Längenmaß, entspricht 30,4 cm*
7 gleaming: strahlend
8 to spread out: ausbreiten
9 recess: Nische
10 guide: Führer
11 entrance: Eingang
12 goblet: Kelch

"So it wasn't stolen," says Peter. "Or it has already been found and returned again."
Bob closes the booklet angrily. He can't bear[1] information that is out of date.
But Justus says, "Neither nor. It's a copy. A reproduction[2]."
"How do you know that?" Peter asks.
"It says so here," Justus says and steps aside to uncover the sign in front of which he has been standing.
"Reproduction by S. Manning, Los Angeles," Bob reads. "You're right!"
He opens his booklet[3] again and compares the statue with the picture. "She really looks exactly like the original."
Peter looks around the room and points to a showcase[4] containing newspaper clippings[5]. "Let's take a look."
Most articles are about successful exhibitions, the high number of visitors and the guests of honor. But there is one which is faded. It deals with the theft of the Madonna.
"On Monday night, unknown culprits[6] stole a valuable[7] Madonna statue from the exhibition[8] room at the Arts and Crafts Museum. The thieves made use of a three minute failure[9] of the surveillance and lighting system[10]. How they got into the building is still unknown. As only one object was stolen, the police believe that it was a continuation[11] of a series of

1 to bear: ertragen
2 reproduction: Nachbildung
3 booklet: Broschüre
4 showcase: Schaukasten
5 newspaper clipping: Zeitungsausschnitt
6 culprit: Täter, Schuldiger
7 valuable: wertvoll
8 exhibition: Ausstellung
9 failure: Ausfall
10 surveillance and lighting system: Überwachungs- und Beleuchtungssystem
11 continuation: Fortsetzung

thefts[1] that began twelve years ago with the theft of an ebony[2] box belonging to Francisco Pizarro [1475-1541]. Every year only one valuable object is stolen. As in past years, the well known collector and patron of arts, the logistics dealer Roger Pen- [continued on page 12]"

The Three Investigators look through the whole paper but there is no page 12.

"Interesting," Justus says. "Look at the name!"

"Roger Pen? What's with the name?"

"Well, it's not complete. And don't you remember what Inspector Cotta told us? That José worked for a logistics company until six months ago. The name of the owner was Pentecost!"

"Right," says Bob. "If José's ex-boss really is the collector and patron of arts, I'm not surprised that Cotta banned us from talking to him. A man like that doesn't want to be bothered[3]."

"Which won't prevent us from bothering[4] him all the same."

"If I am not mistaken we now have a connection between José's Madonna and the statue here," Justus says.

"With a little difference," says Peter. "This one isn't black. Such a good copist ... "

"Copyist."

"– oh, well, someone like that wouldn't observe every detail and then forget the color."

"True, but we'll solve that problem, too. Let's look around and find out what else has been stolen."

"Good idea," says Bob. "If this series of thefts[5] has occurred regularly, then at least ten objects must have disappeared[6] by now."

1 theft: Diebstahl
2 ebony: Ebenholz
3 bothered: gestört
4 to bother: belästigen
5 theft: Diebstahl
6 to disappear: verschwinden

They leave the hall and start the tour again. This time they find the words, "Reproduction by S. Manning, Los Angeles" under several statues and sculptures. All of these replicas had been manufactured[1] in the last ten years and each one replaced a stolen piece of art.
"So, whoever S. Manning is, he's quite talented," Bob says. "I'd never think that all these works of art come from the same artist."
Justus reminds them, "We have dealt with art forgers[2] several times already. Their style must be so brilliant that it doesn't give away their work as a forgery."
"Is it still a forgery, when the original was stolen and the copy is legally reproduced to be put up instead?" Peter asks.
"That's beyond my knowledge," says the First Investigator.
"Finally, the day has come where our First Investigator doesn't know everything," Bob jokes. "I'll mark it on my calendar."
Justus punches[3] Bob's shoulder. Bob didn't expect that, loses his balance, trips and grabs hold of a painting for support[4]. Immediately, all the search lights go on and the alarm starts to wail[5]. The door swings[6] shut and the locks fall into place. Barely[7] five seconds later, an inconspicuous[8] side door swings open and four guards storm in with drawn pistols[9]. A little later, Justus, Peter and Bob are led[10] into the office of the Director of the Museum.

1 to manufacture: herstellen
2 forger: Fälscher
3 to punch: boxen
4 support: Unterstützung
5 to wail: heulen
6 to swing shut: zufallen, zuschwingen
7 barely: kaum
8 inconspicuous: unauffällig, unscheinbar
9 with drawn pistols: mit gezückten Pistolen
10 to lead: führen

8 Milena Osborne is a blonde in her late thirties who coldly scrutinizes[1] the three culprits[2] while the guard explains how they set off the alarm.

"Thanks," she replies and looks at the Three Investigators. "Now what do you have to say?"

"That you have an excellent security system," says Justus. "So I find it even more confusing that it's obviously not capable of stopping real criminals."

She raises her eyebrow. "Young man, do you know how expensive a false alarm is?"

"No," says Justus without flinching[3], "But I know that you have a problem here. We are prepared to help you."

Mrs. Osborne takes a deep breath[4]. Justus takes out a business card and passes it to her.

"We're investigators. May I give you our card?"

The Three Investigators
We take on any case
First Investigator Justus Jonas
Second Investigator Peter Shaw
Research and Archives Bob Andrews

"Investigators?" Mrs. Osborne is quite irritated[5]. "That's ridiculous."

"Not at all. We know your colleagues from the county art museum very well from earlier investigations."

Now she looks at the card. "Oh, that's you?"

1 to scrutinize: mustern
2 culprit: Übeltäter/in, Schuldige/r
3 to flinch: zucken
4 to take a deep breath: tief Luft holen
5 irritated: irritiert

Her voice grows a little friendlier. "And you carry out your investigations by tearing down paintings?"
"That was a mistake," says Bob. "Sorry."
"All the same, it gave us the opportunity to find out that your security system works excellently," says Justus.
"How is it possible that despite[1] that, objects keep disappearing[2]?" Furiously, she stares at him. "You may or may not be an investigator, but I won't put up with this insolence[3]. The police deal with these thefts! You have a different problem at the moment!"
"I didn't want to be rude[4]," Justus replies. "I only wanted to ask you a few questions – "
"Four hundred dollars," she interrupts[5] him brusquely[6]. "That's how much this absurd security operation costs. Thanks to the thefts, I have first class guards and you can't imagine how much that costs. When you go, leave your names and addresses with my secretary. And don't plan on coming here again."
Justus sticks out his chin[7], "Yes, Madam. Since we agree, maybe you could now answer a few questions?"
Furiously, she stares at him. Justus stares back. And unexpectedly, she suddenly starts to laugh.
"You don't give up easily. Oh well, what do you want to know?"
Justus smiles. "Nothing much. Who is Roger Pen … something?"
"Pardon?"
"We found an article about him in the showcase," Bob says. "But unfortunately[8] the article stops halfway through that name."
"Really? I didn't notice that. The name is Pentecost."

1 despite: trotzdem
2 to disappear: verschwinden
3 insolence: Frechheit, Anmaßung
4 rude: unhöflich
5 to interrupt: unterbrechen
6 brusquely: brüsk, barsch
7 chin: Kinn
8 unfortunately: leider

"The owner of the logistics company, Pentecost?" asks Justus innocently.
"No, the company is called Great Deliverance[1]."
"But is that a logistics company?"
"Yes, naturally. Mr. Pentecost has organized the transport of our exhibition pieces for years. He is a great art specialist and promoter[2] of our museum."
"What else does he promote?"
"First of all, he publishes a whole lot of articles in his paper, and –"
The Three Investigators are suddenly electrified. Justus bends forward. "In his paper?"
"Yes, the Carino Daily Post," Mrs. Osborne says. "He's a publisher[3]. The Post has an art supplement every Saturday."
"That's very interesting."
Justus hopes that his voice doesn't sound too tense[4]. "And what has he done in connection with the thefts?"
"He has reproductions of the stolen objects made, pays for them and donates[5] them to us. The reproductions are worthless in comparison[6] to the originals, but they still cost a lot of money. We are very grateful to Mr. Pentecost ..."
Mrs. Osborne sighs. "We would be even more grateful if the police caught these thieves at last. It's a mystery how they can always remove objects from the building so quickly."
"How exactly are the thefts carried out[7]?" asks Justus.
"I won't tell you anything about that."
"Ah," says Justus. "Oh well, Thank you. You've helped us a great deal. Come along, guys!"

1 Great Deliverance (*Wortspiel*): großartige Lieferung und Erlösung
2 promoter: Förderer
3 publisher: Herausgeber
4 tense: angespannt
5 to donate: spenden
6 worthless in comparison: wertlos im Vergleich
7 to carry out: durchführen

"With pleasure," Mrs. Osborne answers. "Good bye. And don't forget to leave your addresses with my secretary."
"Sure ... Oh, one more thing," Justus turns around at the door. "Do you know someone named José Santanda by any chance?"
"José?" Mrs. Osborne asks in surprise. "He was one of Mr. Pentecost's drivers, wasn't he? But as far as I know he left the company. Why are you interested in him?"
"Oh, I was just wondering," Justus answers. "Good bye, Mrs. Osborne."
"At least something makes sense! We have a connection between José and the museum!" TR. 09
"I don't know what it means," says Bob.
"Of course," says Peter. "José works for Pentecost, sees the Madonna during a transport, steals it and hides it under his bed. Someone – perhaps this Jeff – finds out about it, throws him into the water and breaks into the flat. The Madonna's gone. Case solved."
"Unfortunately[1], there are a few gaps[2] in your line of reasoning, Second Investigator," says Justus. "We are dealing with a whole series of thefts which began twelve years ago – but at that time José was only about ten years old. No, there are other people behind the thefts. As to the Madonna, why is she black? And more importantly, where is she now?"

They part at the salvage yard[3]. Bob drives Peter home. Justus enters the yard and locks the gate behind him, then he makes his way to the headquarters[4]. The investigators' office, which is a converted trailer[5], is only approachable[6] by the new secret passage or from the open air

1 unfortunately: leider
2 gaps: Lücken
3 salvage yard: Schrottplatz
4 headquarters: Hauptquartier, Zentrale
5 converted trailer: umgebauter Campinganhänger
6 approachable: zugänglich

work shop next to the fence[1]. Justus opens the door of a huge ancient fridge[2] and climbs in. The back wall of the fridge can be slid to one side by pushing a lever[3]. This was the new "cold gate". He slips through and slides the back wall into place again. He climbs into the office. The telephone is ringing. He switches on the light and answers the phone.

"The Three Investigators, Justus Jonas speaking."

"Listen kid," says an angry male voice, which Justus recognizes at once. The man with the clown's mask, who had thrown José into the water! He switches on the answering machine at once[4].

"You got yourself into something that's none of your business. If you're clever, forget about the Madonna."

"What Madonna?" Justus plays clueless.

"Don't be stupid, you know exactly what I'm talking about. We saw you in the museum's parking lot[5]. I warn you, you're on the wrong side. José Santanda is nothing but a slimy small-time thief,[6] who got what he deserved[7]. You'd better not get too near him. Is that clear?"

"Listen, José is our client. You can't prevent[8] us from making investigations."

"I can't?" says the man with an ugly laugh. "Be careful, kiddo. There's a stove pipe[9] on top of a heap[10] of junk in your yard."

1 fence: Zaun
2 fridge: Kühlschrank
3 lever: Hebel
4 at once: sofort
5 parking lot: Parkplatz
6 slimy small-time thief: schmieriger kleiner Dieb
7 to deserve: verdienen
8 to prevent: verhindern
9 stove pipe: Ofenrohr
10 heap: Haufen

Justus frowns[1]. He glances at his home-made periscope[2], which rises through the ceiling of the headquarters.
"Yes ... and?"
The next moment, something crashes above him. Metal squeaks[3] and the periscope is pulled from its fixture[4]. Broken glass and splinters are flying around. Justus is so scared that he drops the telephone and throws himself on the ground. But then he jumps up again and rushes outside. Quicker than ever, he climbs onto an old iron bed frame[5] and from there onto a cast iron stove[6] and then onto a cupboard[7]. Now he is on the same level as the fence. He pushes himself up and peers[8] onto the street. A car with its headlights switched off drives around the corner and disappears.

Detective Question

What did the Three Investigators find out about the mysterious Mr Pentecost? Is he involved in the thefts?

1 to frown: Stirn runzeln
2 periscope: Periskop
3 to squeak: quietschen, kreischen
4 fixture: Halterung
5 bed frame: Bettgestell
6 cast iron stove: Ofenherd aus Gusseisen
7 cupboard: Schrank
8 to peer: spähen

6. Madonna's Curse[1]

TR. 10

"It was a dark green Ford," says Justus a day later, at the headquarters where they are sitting with the remains[2] of the periscope in front of them. "Our clown phoned from the car and shot at the periscope. What do you think – shall we give up the case?"

Bob and Peter stare at him.

"A suggestion[3] like that from you?" asks Peter. "Are you ill? Was there something in your food?"

"I only want to make it clear what we are in for. After all, it was a serious threat. And the guy has accused our client of being a thief."

"Then we should find out if that's true," says Bob.

"But we are dealing with people who won't hesitate to use violence."

"We've often been threatened[4]," says Peter. "Since when has that stopped us? It only proves that we're on the trail of something really big! And I don't see why we should save people without finding out what it's all about."

"Peter's right," Bob says. "We just have to be careful. I don't think we should show our parents the bill for $400 without at least having compensation[5]. For instance, the reward[6] for finding stolen museum pieces."

Justus nods. "I agree[7]. What did your parents say about the newspaper article?"

"Nothing, luckily[8]."

1 curse: Fluch
2 remains: Überreste
3 suggestion: Vorschlag
4 to threaten: bedrohen
5 compensation: Ausgleich, Entschädigung
6 reward: Belohnung
7 to agree: zustimmen
8 luckily: glücklicherweise

Bob goes to the fridge and comes back with three bottles of soft drinks[1], which he distributes[2] among his friends. "The Carino Daily Post doesn't come out here."

"So we'll carry on?"

"Of course."

"Good. What clues[3] do we have to go on?"

"The museum," says Bob. "The chap said they'd seen us near the museum parking lot."

"Not only that – he said *in* the museum parking lot," says Justus. "As far as I remember that was rather empty[4]. Whom did we see there?"

"No clowns at any rate[5]," says Peter. "Only the truck with the –"

"Mammoth," say Bob and Justus in unison[6].

Justus straightens up. "That's right, Second Investigator! A small mammoth was just being transported. We should find out who drove the truck!"

"How? We've been banned from the Arts and Crafts Museum."

"Yes, but the mammoth doesn't belong to the Arts and Crafts, but to the George C. Page Museum. And we're not banned from that!"

"I just remembered that the Page Museum was also mentioned in the reports about the thefts which I found in the archives today," says Bob and pulls a note from his pocket. "So, twelve years ago a series of thefts took place. All thefts happened at night. The alarm system and the video cameras always shut off for a short time – inside as well as outside, and not only the cameras of the Arts and Crafts, but also those of the Page Museum. The suspicion[7] fell on the museum employees who were on duty at night. However, they all had an alibi."

1 soft drinks: Erfrischungsgetränke
2 to distribute: verteilen
3 clue: Hinweis, Anhaltspunkt
4 empty: leer
5 at any rate: jedenfalls, keinesfalls
6 in unison: einstimmig
7 suspicion: Verdacht

"Hm, for how long did the video cameras fail?" asks Justus.
"Mostly no longer than 2 to 3 minutes."
"That means the stolen objects must have been hidden in the museum so that the thief could get them later."
"The museum was turned upside down after each theft. Nothing was ever found." "Interesting," Justus says. "That means someone had a foolproof[1] method of hiding the stolen objects in the shortest time. Do you have the names of the museum employees?"
"Only those who have already worked there for twelve years and that's at least 10."
Bob glances at his piece of paper. "John Mackenzie, Susan Hamilton, Steve Bright, Leo DiMarco, Brent Smith ..."
"Brent Smith?" Justus sits up. "That could be our B.S., damn – we should have known that yesterday!"
"A museum employee working freelance for the Carino Daily Post?" Peter asks doubtfully.
"Why not?" says Bob. "By the way, I also looked for our talented artist, S. Manning. The artist is a lady called Sybil Manning and lives in the north of Los Angeles."
"Very good, Bob," says Justus.
"And how will we find José's Madonna again as long as we are not sure it's the one which was stolen from the museum?" Peter asks.
"Can't we just visit José and ask him?"
"Do you think José would admit[2] such a thing? He probably already regrets[3] having gotten you involved."
"In case he's woken up in the meantime[4]," says Bob, "should we now visit the various addresses?"
Justus shakes his head. "No, we still need some information about the break-in on Laguna Street, and I know who can give it to us."

1 foolproof: bombensicher
2 to admit: zugeben
3 to regret: bereuen
4 in the meantime: inzwischen

Laguna Street looks just as dreary[1] and unappealing as on their first visit. A few young Mexicans observe the Three Investigators as they walk along the street and stop at number 46. Justus presses the bell.

When the door opens, a small thin man stands in front of them. He is only wearing an undershirt and track pants with slippers[2] on his feet. They recognize him at once and he recognizes them, too. He widens his eyes and slams the door shut[3]. Quick as lightning, Justus puts his foot in the frame.

"Wait! Señor Gonzales."

"Quick, Fernanda," the man calls out in Spanish into the corridor. "The burglars! Call the police!"

"Don't call the police!" Justus calls. "We are not burglars! We only want to talk to you! We are José's friends!"

The Mexican snuffs. "No, you're not! He has no gringos[4] as friends! I've never seen you! Go away! Fernanda!"

"Oh, you've never seen us?" Peter calls angrily. "You said something quite different to the police!"

"Listen," Justus lowers his voice. "It's about a Madonna; do you know something about it?"

This time the man really looks shocked.

"No!"

He wants to push Justus away, but the First Investigator pushes against the door with all his weight[5] and stands still.

"José asked us to bring the Madonna to safety[6], but she was stolen. We think you saw something. Who are you so frightened of[7], Sir? Not us, surely? We can help you!"

1 dreary: trostlos
2 slippers: Pantoffeln, Hausschuhe
3 to slam the door shut: die Türe zuknallen
4 gringo: Gringo *(Mexikanischer Ausdruck für* Weiße/r*)*
5 weight: Gewicht
6 safety: Sicherheit
7 frightened of: sich fürchten vor

The little man shakes his head with despair[1] in his eyes. "Go away, please."
"Do you know who stole the statue? Did you see anyone?"
"I can't tell you anything," the Mexican repeats. "I can't trust you –"
"Nonsense," Justus says impatiently. "We are investigators, not criminals! We are trying to help José!"
Now the man stops resisting[2] at last. His shoulders sag[3] and he only looks tired and bitter. "If you want to help him, don't look for the statue. It would be better if she remained hidden forever."
"Why's that?" Bob asks surprised.
"Because she's evil[4]," Gonzales whispers. "I shouldn't say that, after all she's the Mother of God .... But this statue is evil. She's angry because she was stolen and she poisoned[5] José and only brought him bad luck. I think she will kill him ... and anyone else who touches[6] her wrongfully. And if you look for her, you will also be in harm's way[7]."
The three stare at him aghast[8]. Gonzales turns around, darts[9] into his flat[10], and shuts the door behind him.

Detective Question

Is there an evil curse on the Madonna statue?

1 despair: Verzweiflung
2 to resist: Widerstand leisten, widerstreben
3 to sag: herabsinken
4 evil: böse
5 poisoned: vergiftet
6 to touch: berühren
7 in harm's way: in Gefahr
8 aghast: entgeistert
9 to dart: eilen
10 flat: Wohnung

7. Bob Drops Out[1]

TR. 11

"Of course, all that is pure superstition[2]," Justus explains on the way to the bus stop. "It's just a piece of wood! There's nothing evil about that!"

"Oh, well," says Peter uncomfortably. "But José really did get sick."

"There's probably a natural reason for that."

"But Justus, think about it. If these statues can perform miracles in Europe or elsewhere, then they could also make someone ill."

Justus sighs. "Peter, the statues don't do that! If these cures[3] exist, then only because people strongly believe that they will be cured!"

"Well that's all well and good, but what happens when people believe so strongly that they become sick?"

"Then it's a problem," Justus replies. "But I don't believe in that at all and because of that, nothing will happen to us."

"Nice of you to include[4] us," murmurs Peter.

They take the bus which brings them to the parking lot where they left the VW-Beetle. They look for the address of the logistics company Great Deliverance in an internet café. The company is in Irvine, a part of Los Angeles near Carino Beach. The Three Investigators make their way there immediately, but they soon realize that they are being followed[5]. A row[6] of flashy[7] cars grabs the first opportunity[8] to overtake[9] them. Only one car stays behind.

"A dark green Ford," says Justus. "Somehow I don't think it's a coincidence. Can you try to shake him off, Bob?"

1 to drop out: ausfallen
2 superstition: Aberglaube
3 cure: Heilung
4 to include: einbeziehen
5 followed: verfolgt
6 row: Reihe
7 flashy: auffallend
8 opportunity: Gelegenheit
9 to overtake: überholen

"With the Beetle? Are you joking?"
"I know one of the guys," Peter announces, turning around again. "That's one of the clowns – the one with the blond crew cut. I would recognize the ugly T-shirt anywhere!"
"Then perhaps that's our anonymous[1] telephone caller. Peter, can you recognize the number plate[2]?"
Peter cranes[3] his neck.
"They don't have one. But they have a pistol!" He shouts and throws himself down. "Get down!"
Before Justus and Bob can react, there is a bang. The VW-Beetle shakes as if it has driven up against a curb, and then it drops down in the back on the left. The next moment, the green Ford turns into a side street and zooms off[4] with screeching tyres.[5]
Bob, who is as white as a sheet[6], steers[7] the VW-Beetle to the side of the road and stops.
"They shot the tyre to pieces! Are you OK, Peter?"
"Yes, of course!"
Peter re-emerges. "Justus?"
"I'm OK."
Still trembling, they get out and look at the damage[8]. The right back tyre is completely torn.
"I think I'm calling it a day[9]." says Bob. "I have to have the car towed away[10] and the tyre repaired because the spare tyre[11] has been broken for some time. That's it for me this afternoon."
Justus nods. "Then Peter and I will take the bus."

1 anonymous: anonym
2 number plate: Nummernschild
3 to crane: recken
4 to zoom off: davonbrausen
5 screeching tyres: quietschende Reifen
6 as white as a sheet (*Redewendung*): weiß wie ein Laken
7 to steer: steuern, lenken
8 damage: Schaden
9 to call it a day (*Redewendung*): Feierabend machen
10 to tow away: abschleppen
11 spare tyre: Reserverad

In the late afternoon, after Bob has taken the VW-Beetle to the garage, he cycles to the salvage yard[1] to develop the photos he took at the festival.
Five photos are already drying on the line, three more are darkening in the developer[2] when the trailer starts swaying[3]. Someone is coming in. That must be Justus and Peter, and they are probably quiet because they weren't able to find out anything new from Mr. Pentecost.
"I'm in the dark room[4]," he calls out loudly. "Don't come in!"
They don't answer, but the trailer sways again. The developing liquid[5] splashes about in the bath. In the red light, it looks like thin blood.
Bob frowns. It isn't like Justus and Peter to not say anything at all, even if they have been unsuccessful.
"Justus?" he calls out.
There is still no answer. Instead, the door opens. In the semi-dark, Bob cannot recognize who is standing there. But he ignores him and hastily[6] closes the bag with the photographic paper.
"Look out, man!" He shouts angrily. "You're spoiling all my photos!"
"Quiet!"
The shadowy[7] figure, which he thought to be Justus or Peter, steps forward and then Bob feels something hard and cold at his throat[8].
"Don't move," a hoarse[9] voice whispers.

Detective Question

Who do you think has come to see Bob at the trailer?

1 salvage yard: Schrottplatz
2 developer: Entwickler
3 to sway: schwanken
4 dark room: Dunkelkammer
5 liquid: Flüssigkeit
6 hastily: hastig
7 shadowy: schattenhaft
8 throat: Kehle, Hals
9 hoarse: heiser

8. Great Deliverance

TR. 12

The 'Great Deliverance' warehouse is easy to find. A six foot wall with barbed wire[1] surrounds a fancy[2] villa with a front garden. There are six trucks parked in the yard. The gate, an impressive construction, is engraved[3] with the initials R.P. Justus presses the bell[4]. With a hum[5], the gate slides to one side. When they get to the front door, it also opens with a hum, and Mr. Pentecost is standing in front of them.
He is at most[6] five foot tall and is wearing a dark suit and tie. He has short arms and legs and almost no neck. His head looks as if he never had any hair. He smiles at them, but his stare[7] remains cold.
His deep voice echoes in the hall[8]. "And who are you, if I may ask?"
Justus keeps cool. "Hello, Mr. Pentecost. I'm Justus Jonas, and this is my friend and colleague Peter Shaw. We are investigators. Here's our card."
"Investigators, eh? Then come in."
Mr. Pentecost closes the door and leads Justus and Peter into a room that takes their breath away. It is nearly twelve feet high with two huge glass windows. The floor is made of light, glittering marble[9]. Four very modern white leather chairs are placed around a round glass table on which there is a tray[10] with glasses and drinks. However, it's not the expensive furnishings[11] that amaze Justus and Peter, but rather the statues.

1 barbed wire: Stacheldraht
2 fancy: modisch, protzig
3 engraved: eingraviert
4 bell: Klingel
5 hum: Summen
6 at most: höchstens
7 stare: starrer Blick
8 hall: Flur, Korridor
9 light, glittering marble: heller glänzender Marmor
10 tray: Tablett
11 furnishing: Einrichtung

There are at least 100 figures of women on the walls, some only one and a half feet and others more than 9 feet tall. There are long-legged African figures made of black wood, Asian puppets[1], Indian, Greek and Roman goddesses[2], icons[3], an ancient headless mother goddess, strange round modern sculptures, and three carved[4] European Madonnas.

"Well?" asks Mr. Pentecost. "Do you like them?"

"They are standing too close together," Justus comments critically. "Each one should have enough room so that you can see them properly."

"Right. But then, I would have to have them all over the house and wouldn't have them all around me."

Mr. Pentecost bends forward and pours fruit juice into two glasses which he offers to Justus and Peter. "Now, tell me why you came."

"We want to ask you about a former employee[5]," Justus answers. "José Santanda. He was your driver, wasn't he?"

"Yes, that's right. But unfortunately, I had to dismiss[6] him."

"Have you heard what happened to him?"

"Yes, awful. The world is full of evil."

"The police told us that you would employ him again once he recovers."

"Yes, that's right. You seem to have good police contacts. I think I've heard of you. Have you ever been in the newspaper?"

"Yes," says Justus. "Last Sunday, in the Carino Daily Post, of which you are the publisher. One of your reporters accused[7] us of breaking into[8] José's flat."

1 puppets: Handpuppen, Marionetten
2 goddess: Göttin
3 icon: Ikone
4 carved: geschnitzt
5 former employee: ehemalige/r Angestellte/r
6 to dismiss: entlassen, fortschicken
7 accused: beschuldigt
8 to break into a flat: in eine Wohnung einbrechen

Mr. Pentecost frowns[1]. "How annoying[2]! And it's not true?"
"No, it's not. At least, it's not true that Peter first rescued[3] José and then took his key."
"But it's true that you were in the flat?"
Justus leans back, "It's not important whether we were in the flat or not. The fact is that your reporter B.S. slandered[4] us. By the way[5], what's his full name?"
"Sorry," says Mr. Pentecost, shaking[6] his head. "I don't know all the Carino Daily Post freelance reporters."
"I understand," says Justus politely. "We've also found out that you are not only a publisher and art collector, but also a generous donor[7] to the Arts and Crafts Museum. You've paid for all those reproductions which were made after the thefts. Is that right?"
"That's right," Mr. Pentecost says after a short pause. "I'm a great art lover and I don't like the idea that the public[8] would have to do without the pleasure[9] of these works of art."
"Oh," says Justus. "And how did you do that? I mean, how did the artist S. Manning know what the pieces of art looked like? After all, they were stolen."
"That's not difficult to explain. The museum photographs and catalogs every exhibition piece as soon as it is taken out of the freight[10] container."
"Excuse me?" says Peter. "I – ah – have to go ..."
"Of course," says Mr. Pentecost. "Down the hall on the left."

1 to frown: die Stirn runzeln
2 annoying: ärgerlich
3 to rescue: retten
4 to slander: verleumden
5 by the way (*Redewendung*): übrigens
6 to shake: schütteln
7 generous donor: großzügiger Spender, Förderer
8 public: Öffentlichkeit
9 pleasure: Genuss, große Freude
10 freight: Fracht

Peter stands up and leaves[1] quickly. He really has to go to the toilet, but he is also glad to get away from the statues and their eyes. He takes his time in the restroom. He is in no hurry[2] to go back to the statues or to Mr. Pentecost. He doesn't like the man, but can't say why exactly. There is really no reason to mistrust[3] him. He is José's former employer and wants to help him. So he is one of the good guys.

But he has made a mistake by saying that he doesn't know all the freelance journalists. Justus was only speaking about employees, not about freelancers. When he is finished, he comes out and hesitates[4] in the hall for a moment. Then he notices a beaded curtain[5] which seems to divide the corridor. When he pulls it aside, there are three doors. Perhaps he can find out something while Justus is diverting[6] the art collector. Behind the first door there is a bedroom, behind the second a library, and the third door is locked. Peter bends down and peers[7] through the keyhole. His gaze[8] falls onto a desk. That has to be the office. But that's strange ... Why should Mr. Pentecost lock up his office while he is at home? Because he has visitors, he suddenly thinks, and he might want to be sure that they won't snoop[9] around. Because he knew who we were before Justus told him. Then he also knows why I am not coming back quickly.

Peter swallows[10]. He suddenly realizes how still it is in the house. There is no music or ticking of a clock, it's as silent as a grave[11].

1 to leave: gehen, verlassen, lassen
2 hurry: Eile
3 to mistrust: misstrauen
4 to hesitate: zögern
5 beaded curtain: Perlenvorhang
6 to divert: ablenken
7 to peer: spähen, forschend blicken
8 gaze: Blick
9 to snoop: schnüffeln
10 to swallow: schlucken
11 as silent as a grave: Grabesstille

Suddenly the office phone rings. Peter flinches. After ringing three times it switches to voicemail[1]. When the recording[2] finishes, he hears a distorted[3] voice: "Mr. Pentecost. Smith here. Sheffers has fetched[4] the delivery[5]. I'm driving out this evening." There is a click.
The hair on Peter's neck stands on end[6]. He knows that voice. Not all that long ago he heard it on the headquarters' answering machine.
"Just the name Sheffers?" Justus asks when they are back on the bus. "So not Jeff? Are you sure?"
"Absolutely. He said 'Sheffers has fetched the delivery. I'm going there tonight.' And it was definitely the guy who threw José into the water and threatened us!"
"Very good!"
Justus pats him on the shoulder. "So Pentecost is involved! Did you notice that he made a mistake by talking about the freelance journalist? There must be some proof[7] hidden in his office, otherwise he wouldn't have locked the door when he realized[8] we were coming. We have to get in there somehow!"
"Are you crazy?" Peter bursts out[9]. "He knows who you are! And that's exactly what he expects us to do!"
"Maybe," Justus answers. "But first of all, we'll take on Mr. Sheffers. When Mr. Smith goes there tonight, we'll go, too."

Detective Question

Why does the generous Mr Pentecost also know the reporter? And what is hidden in his locked office?

1 voicemail: Anrufbeantworter auf Mailbox
2 recording: Aufnahme
3 distorted: verzerrt
4 to fetch: holen
5 delivery: Lieferung
6 hair stands on end (*Redewendung*): Haare stehen zu Berge
7 proof: Beweis/e
8 to realize: begreifen
9 to burst out: herausplatzen

9. José Backs Out

TR. 13

But things turn out differently. When they finally climb out of the bus and go up the winding[1] street to Titus Jonas' salvage yard, the sun is setting[2] and the houses are throwing long shadows[3]. They climb through the green gate into the outside workshop[4] and stop short. The door to Headquarters is open. Someone inside is talking, but it isn't Bob. The strange voice sounds angry. Justus and Peter stand still and listen.

"Where the heck[5] are your friends?"

"They must be coming soon," answers Bob.

"You already said that an hour ago. Listen, gringo. I'm not going to let you make a fool[6] of me."

"My name is Bob," says Bob. "And perhaps you'll put away the knife and untie me. I've told you at least twenty times that we only wanted to help you."

"And I say that I don't need your help! You only got me into more trouble[7]! For the last time, where is the Madonna?"

Justus and Peter exchange glances. Justus grabs a rusty metal rod[8], Peter a wooden stick and they storm into the trailer. The visitor turns around. It is a young Mexican in jeans and a T-shirt. He is holding a knife in his hand. Bob is sitting on the chair behind him with his hands and feet bound together.

"Now," Justus says and lifts the rod threateningly[9]. "Drop the knife!"

1 winding: kurvenreich, kurvig
2 the sun is setting: die Sonne geht unter
3 shadow: Schatten
4 workshop: Werkstatt
5 where the heck (*Umgangssprache*): wo zum Teufel
6 fool: Narr
7 trouble: Schwierigkeiten
8 rusty metal rod: rostige Eisenstange
9 threateningly: drohend

The stranger hesitates, glances at Bob, shrugs his shoulders and lets go of the knife. It falls onto the ground and its blade[1] digs into the floor.
"Bob, is everything OK?"
"Sure," Bob answers. "May I introduce[2] you? This is our client. José Santanda."
"Excuse me?" says an astonished[3] Justus.
Peter, who wants to push past the visitor, looks at him properly for the first time.
"José? I didn't recognize you at all! Why did you tie Bob up and threaten him? Are you crazy?"
"Me?" José gives him a hostile[4] look. "I could ask you the same. How dare you poke your nose into my business?"
Now, Justus is left speechless[5].
"Hold on a minute," protests Peter at once. "You begged[6] me to bring the Madonna to safety so that the clowns wouldn't get her!"
"What have I? You're mad[7], all of you! What did you do with her?"
"Would someone finally untie[8] me, please!" Bob calls out furiously.
"I'm coming!" Peter pushes past José, pulls the knife out of the floor and cuts through Bob's ropes.
"Listen," says José. "I don't know who you are, but I certainly did not give you an order. OK? I only want you to give up the Madonna and then forget you ever heard of me."
"How often must we tell you that we don't have it!" Bob shouts. "Justus, you tell him, perhaps he'll believe you!"

1 blade: Klinge
2 to introduce sb: jemanden vorstellen
3 astonished: erstaunt, verblüfft
4 hostile: feindselig, ablehnend
5 speechless: sprachlos
6 to beg: betteln
7 mad: verrückt
8 to untie: losbinden

"We really don't have it," Justus leans the metal rod against the wall and sits down. "When we arrived in the flat, she was gone and the whole place was ransacked."
"Gonzales already told me that." José's expression remains as sinister as before. "And what did you intend to do with the statue? You don't just put something like that into someone's flat."
"Mr. Pentecost does," says Justus and watches him intently[1]. "Because we visited him this afternoon."
José is visibly[2] shocked. "Pentecost? And what did you tell him?"
"Nothing. Why? What should we have told him?"
This time José avoids[3] his gaze[4]. "Oh, nothing. So what did you plan on doing with the Madonna?"
"We don't know that," says Peter. "You said 'Bring her ...' and then you collapsed. Where should we have brought her to?"
"If you don't know where she is, that's it for you. Don't ever interfere in my business again, OK?"
He takes the knife off the table where Peter left it and angrily puts it into his pocket.
"Sit down," Justus orders[5]. And when José doesn't move, he gets up and pushes him into the chair. "Perhaps you'd at least[6] like to hear what we've found out."
"No, I don't." But José stays where he is, screws up his face and puts his hand over his stomach[7]. He surely doesn't look as well as he claims to be. His face is pale[8] and gaunt[9]. Justus sits on the corner of the desk.

1 intently: aufmerksam
2 visibly: sichtbar
3 to avoid: vermeiden
4 gaze: (starrer) Blick
5 to order: befehlen
6 at least: wenigstens, zumindest
7 stomach: Bauch, Magen
8 pale: blass
9 gaunt: ausgemergelt

"After you asked Peter to get the Madonna, we went to your flat and found it completely ransacked[1]. The clowns had already been there and fled[2], but they did not carry a statue. Tonio Gonzales later told the police he hadn't seen the four guys, but described[3] us. He even described Bob's glasses although he wasn't wearing them."

José glances at Bob, but remains silent[4]. Justus continues: "Until six months ago, you worked for a logistics company called Great Deliverance. Your boss is called Pentecost and he said he'd like to employ you again when you're better."

He stops when José laughs out loud.

"What's so funny?"

"Nothing, did he really say that? He'd like to employ me again?"

"Yes. Who is Smith?"

Justus hopes to catch José unawares[5], but it doesn't work. The Mexican's pale face turns expressionless[6].

"Who?"

"The guy who threw you into the water. And the man who left a message on our answering machine[7] and accused you of being a thief."

"And the man who phoned Mr. Pentecost today and told him that someone called 'Sheffers' fetched a delivery," said Peter. "So, Smith apparently[8] works for Pentecost. Then we have to ask ourselves why Pentecost so charmingly assured[9] the police that he would like to employ you again. If at the same time, he sent some guys after you to kill you."

José remains silent.

1 ransacked: durchwühlt, geplündert
2 to flee: flüchten
3 to describe: beschreiben
4 to remain silent: stillbleiben
5 unawares: unaufmerksam
6 expressionless: ausdruckslos
7 answering machine: Anrufbeantworter
8 apparently: offensichtlich, anscheinend
9 to assure: versichern, vergewissern

"Did you steal the Madonna from him?" Justus asks abruptly. "His whole living room is full of statues – was she one of them?"
"No. She was lying in the attic[1]."
José gets up with difficulty and grits his teeth[2] for a moment as if he is in a lot of pain.
"I thought she was worthless[3]. And she made me ill. I wanted you to give her back to him – nothing more. I wanted to have peace[4] and I wish I'd never touched[5] the thing."
"How can a statue make you ill?" asks Bob. "You don't believe that she is cursed[6], do you?"
"Ah, did Gonzales tell you about the curse?" José forces a grin. "Yes, he believes something like that."
"And you don't?" Justus asks.
José only shrugs his shoulders[7] and goes to the door.
"What does the statue look like?" asks Justus.
"That doesn't matter now."
"No, wait a minute. She's still missing and we can help you."
José doesn't even answer anymore. He leaves the place, slowly climbs[8] over the iron fence and walks away.

Detective Question

Why is Bob tied up by José Santanda? And does José also believe in the curse of the Madonna?

1 attic: Dachboden
2 to grit one's teeth: Zähne knirschen
3 worthless: wertlos
4 peace: Frieden
5 to touch: berühren
6 to be cursed: verflucht sein
7 to shrug one's shoulders: mit den Schultern zucken
8 to climb: klettern

10. A Bad Mistake[1]

TR. 14

Once José has left, Bob goes into the dark room to look at the photos. Some are spoiled[2]. He spreads[3] the rest on to the table.
"Pentecost!" Justus bursts out. "You photographed Pentecost!"
"What?" Bob bends forward. "Where?"
"The little fat one there, behind the stand. He's talking to a trader."
"And I know who the trader is," Peter says. "That's the passenger[4] from the car that followed us, the one with the pistol."
Justus' eyes begin to sparkle. "Are you quite sure?"
"Absolutely. I told you I recognized the blond crew cut and the guy's white T-shirt."
"Very good," says Justus. "So we have a very wealthy[5] logistics entrepreneur[6], collector and promoter of art who sends off four men to force a small-time thief to return something to him. Meanwhile, he doesn't hesitate to inflict harm, or commit burglary or damage property. What do we conclude from that?"
"That the Madonna is very important to him."
"That she's not nearly as worthless as José thinks."
"I still don't understand that," says Bob. "Why does José steal the statue of a Madonna which he thinks is worthless, when he knows that Pentecost collects statues like that?"
"Perhaps there's something valuable[7] hidden[8] inside? Maybe gold?" Peter suggests.

1 mistake: Fehler
2 spoiled: verdorben
3 to spread: ausbreiten
4 passenger: Beifahrer
5 wealthy: wohlhabend, reich
6 entrepreneur: Unternehmer
7 valuable: wertvoll
8 hidden: versteckt

"Or a treasure map[1]? She's rather old and could have a secret compartment[2]."
"Could be, but I don't think so," Justus says. "Let's suppose it's really a statue from the museum, then we could prove Pentecost's involvement[3] in the thefts. And of course, he's afraid of that."
"But it's not the same statue. She's black – not colored."
"Yes, I've noticed that as well. But there must be some evidence[4] for my theory. I'd love to know what Pentecost is hiding in his study – perhaps that would get us further."
"But we don't have a client anymore," Bob interrupts.
"That's a formality," Justus says.
"No, José doesn't want us to interfere in his business. He's probably had even more trouble[5] with Pentecost because of us. We should keep out of it."
"In any case, he's only waiting for us to turn up[6]," Peter says.
"I don't think so," Justus says. "And have you realized that maybe José wants to get rid of[7] us because he's still afraid of Pentecost? But we promised[8] to help him." He glances at his watch.
"Half past nine. It's best if you come here at 2 o'clock. And bring your skeleton key, Peter."
Peter and Bob stare at him. They are used to Justus taking the lead in dubious matters[9], but they have not been treated[10] so rudely in a long time.
"Did you hear what we said?"

1 treasure map: Schatzkarte
2 secret compartment: Geheimfach
3 involvement: Beteiligung, Verwicklung
4 evidence: Beweis, Indiz
5 trouble: Ärger, Probleme
6 to turn up (*Umgangssprache*): auftauchen
7 to get rid of sb: jemanden loswerden
8 to promise: versprechen
9 matters: Angelegenheiten
10 to treat: behandeln

"Of course," says Justus. "See you later."
"Oh no," says Bob. "That doesn't work for me anymore, Justus Jonas. Perhaps you've already forgotten the trouble we had with Inspector Cotta because of Laguna Street. Not me! If José doesn't exonerate[1] us, we'll be charged with burglary! We can't always climb into other people's houses!"
"Then you want to let José down?"
"He doesn't want us to help him!"
"Another reason[2] for us to find out what's really up."
"No," says Bob decidedly[3].
"Without me. If we can't do our investigations legally, we have to rethink[4] our investigation work."
He gets up. "Or at least you should do that. For me, it's pretty clear and I'm not breaking in anywhere. Goodnight. See you tomorrow! Coming, Peter?"
Peter nods. "Night, Justus."
"Fine," Justus says furiously[5]. "Then I'll go alone."
"Do what you want! Bye."
It rarely happens that Bob slams the door of the headquarters behind him, but he does this time.

Justus Jonas, however[6], doesn't let anyone talk him out of a plan easily. In the middle of the night, a taxi drives through Irvine and stops two streets away[7] from Great Deliverance's grounds. Justus gets out. He waits until the taxi disappears and then continues on his way. The moon is high in the sky and throws a white, unreal light over the

1 to exonerate: entlasten
2 reason: Grund
3 decidedly: entschieden
4 to rethink: überdenken
5 furiously: wütend
6 however: jedoch
7 away: entfernt

empty[1] street and the high wall which surrounds the property[2] of the company. Justus creeps to the gate. Of course it is locked.
Suddenly he hears steps. The door of a car opens and closes again. He swiftly[3] hides in the shadows[4] of the gate. A car slowly rolls up to the gate and turns on its headlights[5], which blind Justus. He squeezes his eyes shut, but he still recognizes the car. It is the dark green Ford. That is no longer a surprise, because they know that Pentecost is working with the clowns. Who is driving? And what does he want to do in the middle of the night? Is this related to the delivery which Smith mentioned on the phone?

The gate slides open soundlessly and the car drives through. Now or never! Before the gate closes, Justus makes a run for it[6] and throws himself behind a bush in the garden. The passengers don't seem to notice[7] anything. The car drives off and the gate closes with a click. Justus gets up and creeps towards the house. Pentecost seems to rely on his electric gate[8], the high walls, and the barbed wire[9] because a window on the ground floor is ajar[10]. Justus looks around. In the moonlight, the garden seems deserted[11]. And no one in the street can look in. He quickly pushes the window open and climbs into the house. TR. 15

1 empty: leer
2 property: Gelände, Besitz
3 swiftly: schnell, geschwind
4 shadow: Schatten
5 headlight: Scheinwerfer
6 to make a run for it (*Redewendung*): abhauen
7 to notice: bemerken
8 gate: Tor
9 barbed wire: Stacheldraht
10 to be ajar: angelehnt sein, einen Spalt offen stehen
11 deserted: verlassen

He finds himself in the library[1] that Peter told him about. His flashlight[2] lights up hundreds of arts and reference books. Justus tiptoes[3] to the door. Everything is quiet. Will the study door be locked? Hardly – if Pentecost is on his own. Justus tries the latch[4] and the door opens. The study is chaotic, but it looks like an organized chaos. There is a big oak[5] desk by the window, and in the corner there's a modern table with a computer and printer on it. Both the desk and the table are stacked[6] high with papers, files, pictures, newspapers, magazines and only a tiny working space[7] is left empty. Next to the door there is a locked old oak cupboard in front of which hundreds of newspapers are piled[8] up high, just like on the book shelves next to it. The room is a strange contrast to the sterile emptiness of the hall and the living room in which the only life were the statues.
Justus darts[9] to the desk and sits down. He looks at the high pile of records[10], mainly files[11] from the logistics company, but also 'Thank you letters' from the Arts and Crafts Museum for further donations[12] of a reproduction and a file headed[13] "C.D.P." Carino Daily Post! Justus opens the file and shines his flashlight on it. The first thing he finds is the article about the Three Investigators written by B.S. Under the computer print out,[14] there is a handwritten commentary:

1 library: Bibliothek
2 flashlight: Taschenlampe
3 to tiptoe: schleichen, auf Zehenspitzen gehen
4 latch: Türschloss
5 oak: Eiche
6 stacked: gestapelt
7 working space: Arbeitsplatz
8 piled: gestapelt
9 to dart: stürzen, sausen
10 record: Akte
11 file: Ordner, Datei
12 further donations: weitere Spenden
13 headed: mit der Überschrift
14 print out: Ausdruck

I asked a colleague about the three boys. They are called Peter Shaw, Bob Andrews and Justus Jonas. They are known as the Three Investigators of Rocky Beach. Their reputation with the police is good because they have often solved minor crime cases on their own. I have written an article which connects[1] them to the burglary. That will give them something to chew on[2] for a while and perhaps[3] they won't cross our paths[4] anymore. If they do, we should think about taking tougher[5] action. Steve Bright.

Steve Bright ... S.B. ... B.S.! Justus turns the pages in the file and indeed[6] the surname is listed first on every article. However, he remembers the name in connection with something else ... What is it? Then he remembers. Steve Bright is the name of one of the employees of the Arts and Crafts Museum. Excitedly, he continues turning the pages, but finds nothing useful[7]. He puts the file back and digs[8] further until suddenly the flashlight shines on a strange grouping of numbers, lines and letters, which he didn't expect on an art collector's desk. He bends over them and tries to decipher[9] the combination. It appears to be a chemical formula. Justus reads the notes[10] below and after a while the hair on the back of his neck stands up on end. That's it! The connection, the solution[11] – which he's been trying to find the whole time!

1 to connect: verbinden
2 to chew on sth (*Redewendung*): an etwas knabbern, etwas verarbeiten
3 perhaps: vielleicht
4 to cross paths: Wege kreuzen
5 tough: rau, zäh
6 indeed: allerdings
7 useful: nützlich
8 to dig: graben
9 to decipher: entschlüsseln, erkennen
10 note: Notiz
11 solution: Lösung

With trembling[1] fingers, he pulls out the sheet of paper and folds it. Just as he is about to put it in his pocket, a voice coming from the door speaks, "I think that's enough. Don't you?"
Justus stops dead. At the same time, a blinding flashlight blazes[2] from the shelf[3], and from the hall another well known and meanwhile despised[4] voice says: "Caught in action. That's going to be a smashing[5] photo, Mr. Pentecost. The Post will be pleased with that!"

Detective Question

Who do you think caught Justus in Mr. Pentecost's office?

1 trembling: zitternd
2 to blaze: grell scheinen
3 shelf: Regal
4 despised: verhasst, verachtenswert
5 smashing (*Umgangssprache*): grandios

11. The End of the Three Investigators

TR. 16

"Very good, Mr. Smith. And tomorrow morning it will not only be in the Carino Daily Post, but also in all the other Los Angeles papers," says Mr. Pentecost, entering[1] the room. He is fully dressed[2], holding a pistol in his hand.

"I'm disappointed[3], Justus Jonas. I didn't think you would be so stupid as to walk into my trap[4]. Obviously, I had hoped you would because this way I can get rid of you troublesome[5] rebels once and for all." He takes a few more steps forward and stretches out his free hand. "Give me that."

Without a word, Justus passes him the slip of paper with the formula. He feels like a real fool for being so stupid. The open gate, the open window had all been so inviting[6], he should have been doubly suspicious.

"Now don't move," Pentecost says. "There are far too many young criminals in this town. The police will be glad to hear that I've caught[7] one of them."

He digs out a telephone from under the pile of letters and dials.

"Oh yes, call the police," Justus says in his most arrogant voice. "I'm sure Inspector Cotta will be interested in what I have found here. I'm an honorary[8] police assistant from Rocky Beach."

1 to enter: hereinkommen
2 dressed: angezogen
3 disappointed: enttäuscht
4 trap: Falle
5 troublesome: lästig, störend
6 inviting: einladend
7 to catch: fangen
8 honorary: ehrenamtlich

"Oh really?" Mr. Pentecost is unimpressed[1]. "That's interesting. Then why don't you show me the search warrant[2] that gives you permission[3] to snoop around my house? As honorary police assistant, you surely know that I could even bring charges against Mr. Inspector Cotta himself for burglary, if he gained entry[4] into my house and took possession[5] of any of my belongings without a judge's authorization[6]. So, if you please?"

He puts the telephone down and once again holds out his hand. He is still holding the pistol in the other one. Justus is somehow thrown off guard[7]. Until now, the Three Investigators had always gotten away with the threat[8] of informing the police!

"I don't have a search warrant," he says. "But I can't imagine that you would really call the police. We know that you told the clowns to intimidate[9] José so he would return[10] the statue and both the men who shot our tyre to bits[11] work with you as well!"

"Oh yes?" Mr. Pentecost sounds bored[12]. "Is that it?"

Justus hesitates. He is very tempted to explain how a juvenile salvage yard investigator has managed to find out Pentecost's plans. However, his instincts warn him against that. Pentecost has already set a gang of dangerous thugs[13] onto him. He has such a great deal to lose that when he realizes what the First Investigator has found out, he probably wouldn't hesitate to do away with Justus altogether.

1 unimpressed: unbeeindruckt
2 search warrant: Durchsuchungsbefehl
3 permission: Genehmigung
4 to gain entry: Einlass erlangen
5 to take possession: in Besitz nehmen
6 a judge's authorization: Ermächtigung von einem Richter
7 off guard: unachtsam, überrumpelt
8 threat: Drohung
9 to intimidate: einschüchtern
10 to return: zurückkehren
11 to shoot to bits: in Stücke zerschießen
12 bored: gelangweilt
13 thug: Schlägertyp

"Yes," he says. "Unfortunately, but I'm sure I'd have found some evidence against you! Probably the whole cupboard is full of grinning clown masks!"

Smith smiles and even Pentecost grins, but both stop grinning as Justus continues.

"And I'm going now. That photo is a bluff. You can't risk calling the police or putting anything into the paper." He doesn't get any further. The pistol in Mr. Pentecost's hand suddenly cracks sharply and hits a piece of stone near Justus' feet. Numb[1] with fear, Justus jumps back as the the gun is aimed[2] at him again.

"My dear young burglar[3]," says Mr. Pentecost and picks up the telephone again. "You're not going anywhere. You'll stay here quietly and wait until the police arrive."

Justus' heart sinks. How could he have fallen into such a trap? And how is he going to get out of it now? Full of despair[4] he tries to think of a way out! But then he hears a sound through the window which he didn't expect or even hope for: The call of the red–breasted flycatcher[5]. It's the secret signal of the Three Investigators. Peter and Bob have arrived. Justus almost grows dizzy[6] with relief.

"May I sit down?" he asks softly and humbly[7].

Pentecost shrugs his shoulders. "I don't care. Smith, search[8] his pockets. Perhaps he's already stolen one or the other crystal vase."

"Certainly not," replies Justus irritably. "You know quite well that I'm not a thief!"

1 numb: gefühllos, taub
2 to aim: zielen
3 burglar: Einbrecher
4 full of despair: verzweifelt
5 red-breasted flycatcher *(Vogelname)*: Zwergschnäpper, Rotbauchfliegenschnäpper
6 dizzy: schwindelig
7 humbly: demütig
8 to search: durchsuchen

"Of course," says Pentecost, smiling at him. "But the police don't know that. I think we can just put one or two items into your bag. And no one will believe you ever again."
Smith comes closer and grabs[1] Justus' bag. Justus had expected that. Quick as lightning, he pushes the bag into Smith's face, jumps up and throws his whole weight[2] against him. The surprised man tumbles backwards into Pentecost's line of fire[3].
"Careful," shouts Pentecost and raises his arm. A shot goes off and Justus doesn't wait to see who or what is hit. He runs to the door and dashes[4] out. The library! If only the window is still open! Behind him, he hears Pentecost shout: "Stop or I'll shoot."
Justus doesn't think of stopping. He storms into the library, runs to the window, pulls it open and swings himself out. Bob is standing outside and Justus nearly falls on top of him[5].
"Justus – what ..."
"Get out of here!" Justus shouts. "Where's Peter?"
"He's opening the gate!"
They run off. At the electric gate, Peter pushes with all his strength[6]. The MG[7] is standing next to it with its engine running[8]. Bob and Justus jump into the small car. Peter accelerates[9] immediately. And with screeching tyres[10] the MG spins[11] out of the driveway into the street and shoots away just as the first police sirens can be heard in the distance[12].

1 to grab: greifen, grabschen
2 weight: Gewicht
3 line of fire: Schusslinie
4 to dash: stürzen
5 nearly falls on top of him: fällt beinahe auf ihn
6 strength: Kraft
7 MG: *Britische Automarke*
8 with its engine running: mit laufendem Motor
9 to accelerate: beschleunigen, Gas geben
10 with screeching tyres: mit quietschenden Reifen
11 to spin: wirbeln
12 distance: Entfernung, Ferne

At half past six, Justus is arrested[1]. At half past eight, an article with a photo of him in Pentecost's office is in all the newspapers. Obviously[2], Mr. Pentecost has mobilized all his contacts. At three o'clock, Aunt Mathilda and Uncle Titus pay the bail[3] and pick Justus up from the police station. TR. 17

Against Justus' expectations[4], Aunt Mathilda says very little during the unending drive home and Uncle Titus says nothing at all. And that is even worse[5]. Only when they get to the salvage yard does Aunt Mathilda turn to Justus and say, "You are grounded[6]. And this old trailer will be thrown out with the next scrap transport. You can remove what you need, but your investigator game is over. Once and for all. Do you understand?"

"But Aunt Mathilda –"

"I said, do you understand, Justus?" Aunt Mathilda seldom[7] speaks in this tone, but whenever she does, cold shivers run up and down his spine[8].

"Yes, Aunty."

"Now, get out."

Justus climbs out of the car and stands there, his head hanging.

"Do I have to go into the house at once?" he asks.

"You are grounded to the house and yard. After all, we need you here to help. But you are not to set a foot outside the gate."

Uncle Titus still hasn't said a word. He waits until his wife gets out, before he drives the car to its parking spot[9], gets out and goes into

1 arrested: verhaftet
2 obviously: offensichtlich
3 bail: Kaution
4 expectation: Erwartung
5 even worse: sogar noch schlimmer
6 to be grounded: Hausarrest haben
7 seldom: selten
8 cold shivers run up and down his spine (*Redewendung*): ihm laufen kalte Schauer über den Rücken
9 parking spot: Parkplatz

his office. Aunt Mathilda goes into the house and Justus creeps into the headquarters. Inside, he looks at the cozy[1] chaos which has been his home in the last years, even more so than his room inside the house. How many cases started here! How often did Peter and Bob sit here discussing the craziest ideas, making plans, and tinkering[2] with technical stuff ... And that was now over? Neither Peter nor Bob has phoned and Justus assumes that their parents have forbidden them to associate with[3] him, the 'burglar'.
And yet, he is so sure that he has solved the case – no, he is still not sure, but the police in Los Angeles are not even slightly[4] interested in what he can tell them about Mr. Pentecost. Because he doesn't have final proof yet, his findings aren't worth[5] very much anyway. Mr. Pentecost made his statement[6] and walked away triumphantly as a free man, while Justus was taken away like a criminal.
Inspector Cotta can't help him either. "Sorry, but it's your own fault. You don't become a burglar for good or bad reasons. You become a burglar as soon as you break in somewhere."
And Justus knows that he is right. That they are all right. But still ...
He sits down at the desk and pulls out the keyboard. At least he wants to look at his e-mail before he dismantles[7] everything. It takes a lot of time for the computer to start up. Justus accesses his e-mail. Spam, spam, spam, Santanda, spam – Santanda!
It's me, José Santanda. I've gone into hiding[8]. Call me back – 323-357-5523. Otherwise, I'm in a fix[9].

1 cozy: gemütlich, behaglich
2 to tinker: basteln, ausprobieren
3 to associate with sb: mit jemandem verkehren
4 not even slightly: nicht im geringsten, kein bisschen
5 worth: wert
6 statement: Aussage
7 to dismantle: etwas zerlegen, auseinanderbauen
8 to go into hiding (*Redewendung*): untertauchen
9 to be in a fix (*Redewendung*): in der Patsche sitzen

Justus automatically looks up at the ceiling where a huge plan of Los Angeles is pinned up. 323 is the area code[1] for Hollywood. Not so far away. He reaches for the telephone and has already dialed the first two digits[2] before he stops. He just stands there for a long time. Soon, the expected silence of the receiver[3] turns into the beeping of the busy signal[4]. Justus listens and stares into space[5]. Then he replaces the receiver. He deletes[6] the e-mail and begins to take the map off the ceiling[7].

Detective Question

Why does Uncle Titus have to bail Justus out of prison? Has Justus turned into a burglar?

1 area code: Vorwahl
2 digit: Ziffer
3 receiver: Hörer
4 busy signal: Besetztzeichen
5 to stare into space: ins Leere starren
6 to delete: löschen
7 ceiling: Zimmerdecke

12. Unexpected Aid[1]

TR. 18

Peter and Bob spend a very unpleasant[2] day at school. The Three Investigators have often been the centre of attention after newspaper reports, but they are rarely avoided[3] so openly and whispered about by the other pupils as they are now. The news that Justus has been imprisoned[4] has spread like a bushfire[5].

They meet during break to talk about the situation.

"I don't understand," says Peter. "Why didn't he tell the police what he found out about Pentecost and the museum? He told us that he had solved the case[6]."

"But he also said that final evidence[7] was still missing[8]. And now look at this," Bob pulls a newspaper article out of his bag; Peter takes it and reads the headline[9].

"Another mysterious theft in the Arts and Crafts Museum! Spanish gold helmet[10] disappeared without a trace[11] – police are puzzled!"

"When was that?"

"Last night," says Bob. "Soon after the green Ford left Pentecost's grounds. Even the time is right – there was a power cut[12] at four o'clock."

1 aid: Hilfe
2 unpleasant: unerfreulich
3 to avoid: vermeiden
4 imprisoned: eingesperrt
5 to spread like bushfire (*Redewendung*): sich verbreiten wie ein Lauffeuer
6 to solve the case: den Fall lösen
7 final evidence: der letzte noch fehlende Beweis
8 missing: fehlend, vermisst
9 headline: Überschrift
10 helmet: Helm
11 trace: Spur
12 power cut: Stromausfall

"We have to show this to Justus," Peter says.
"Then we'll be in more trouble."
Peter sighs. "True."

Justus hasn't decided yet[1] what to say when he goes back to school again. He spends[2] Thursday morning clearing out the dark room. Then he takes the table and bench[3] apart and piles the parts[4] up against the fence. He is just starting to pull the cable out of the computer when he hears Uncle Titus shout, "Justus! You have a visitor[5]."
Quickly he climbs through the headquarters, opens the fridge[6] door and climbs out. A little round Mexican looking woman whom he has never seen before is waiting at the door of Uncle Titus' office. She is wearing a colourful dress and a red headscarf[7].
"That's my nephew[8]," says Uncle Titus. "Justus, this is Señora Fernanda Gonzales. She wants to talk to you." He sounds less obliging[9] than usual[10].
"Thanks, Uncle Titus." He turns to the woman and smiles glumly[11]. "How can I help you?"
Uncle Titus goes back into his office and Señora Gonzales turns to Justus. She talks with a surprisingly energetic voice.
"I read in the paper that you broke in at Mr. Pentecost's and were locked up[12]! Why did you do that?"

1 hasn't decided yet: hat sich noch nicht entschieden
2 to spend: verbringen
3 bench: Sitzbank
4 part: Teil
5 visitor: Besucher
6 fridge (*Abkürzung für* refrigerator): Kühlschrank
7 headscarf: Kopftuch
8 nephew: Neffe
9 obliging: entgegenkommend
10 usual: gewöhnlich, üblicherweise
11 glumly: mürrisch, betreten
12 locked up: eingesperrt

"Investigations," Justus answers curtly[1].

"So you're really investigators?" she laughs a little. "Did you find the statue?"

"No." Justus takes a deep breath. "And I'm sorry I have to tell you that I'm no longer in the investigations business."

"Trouble, hm?" Señora Gonzales nods[2] and throws him an almost furtive[3] glance.

"My husband warned you that looking for the statue would only bring you bad luck[4]."

"That doesn't have anything to do with bad luck, only with bad investigation[5] methods."

This time she really laughs.

"So you're not superstitious[6]?"

"Not in the least," Justus answers with emphasis[7]. "And I have to ask you to leave, I'm afraid I'm busy[8]."

"Yes, of course." She nods[9] again. "What did you want to know from my husband that made him so panicky?"

"That's not important anymore."

"Yes, it is," she says very forcefully[10]. "I don't think one should be afraid. If there's a problem, one has to solve it. And we do have a problem. José phoned and told us that you didn't answer his e-mail. I like the young man very much, and he's a good neighbor, and I refuse to be afraid of a few rascals that count on the fact that out of fear we won't betray[11] them."

1 curtly: brüsk, barsch
2 to nod: nicken
3 furtive: verstohlen
4 bad luck: Pech
5 investigation: Untersuchung
6 superstitious: abergläubig
7 with emphasis: mit Nachdruck, betont
8 busy: beschäftigt
9 to nod: nicken
10 forcefully: energisch
11 to betray: verraten, hintergehen

She taps Justus' chest[1] and says, "I'll help you."
Justus throws a desperate[2] glance at Uncle Titus' office and heroically struggles[3] against temptation[4].
"I told you I'm no longer investigating this case."
"Have your parents forbidden it?"
"They are not – yes, they have forbidden it."
At this strategically unfortunate[5] moment, Aunt Mathilda comes out of the house. "Justus, come in for lunch."
"I'm sorry," Justus says to Señora Gonzales and starts to move. "There's really nothing I can do. Goodbye!"
He goes to the house and sees his aunt looking grimmer[6] and grimmer the closer he gets. He only notices what the cause[7] is when she stares over his shoulder and asks in a threatening[8] voice, "Can I help you, madam?"
He turns around and discovers[9] Fernanda Gonzales, who is following him and is now smiling up at Aunt Mathilda.
"Mrs. Jonas? Yes? I am Fernanda Gonzales. I'm very glad to meet you!"
"Thank you," says Aunt Mathilda curtly.
"Come in, Justus. Your food is getting cold. In case you want to buy something, please go to my husband, who will be pleased –"
"No, thank you. I don't want to buy anything." Señora Gonzales remains friendly. "I want to congratulate[10] you on this very helpful and

1 chest: Brustkorb, Brust
2 desperate: verzweifelt
3 to struggle: ringen, dagegen ankämpfen
4 temptation: Versuchung
5 unfortunate: unglücklich, ungünstig
6 grim: düster, grimmig
7 cause: Grund, Ursache
8 threatening: drohend
9 to discover: entdecken
10 to congratulate: gratulieren

well-mannered boy. I'm sure you have heard how selflessly[1] he and his friends risked their lives for our neighbor. Poor José."
Aunt Mathilda answers reluctantly[2], "Thank you. Come in, Justus."
Justus doesn't wait to see how the meeting goes on. He slips past Aunt Mathilda into the kitchen, where he devours[3] two big hamburgers. He doesn't have much hope; Señora Gonzales will never manage[4] to change his aunt's mind[5]. After about ten minutes, Aunt Mathilda comes into the kitchen and scrutinizes[6] her nephew as if she were seeing him for the first time. Then she goes to the fridge and begins to rummage about[7]. "That's really a very nice lady."
Justus can't believe his ears[8].
"She explained a few things to me," Aunt Mathilda continues and turns around. "I have to say I still don't approve[9] of this investigator game, but I have to admit that you've helped a lot of people."
"Thank you, Aunt Mathilda," Justus answers.
"All the same, I never want to have to fetch you from a police station again."
"No, Aunt Mathilda."
"And if I think about it, we don't need the space near the fence that urgently[10]. And anyway, I don't know what to do with all the junk."
She looks at her nephew with a penetrating gaze. "I'll talk to your uncle about it."

1 selflessly: selbstlos
2 reluctantly: widerstrebend
3 to devour: vertilgen
4 to manage: schaffen
5 to change one's mind: seine Meinung ändern
6 to scrutinize: inspizieren, kritisch blicken
7 to rummage about: herumstöbern, wühlen
8 can't believe his ears: traut seinen Ohren nicht
9 to approve: befürworten, bejahen
10 urgently: dringend

Justus stands up, goes up to his aunt, and hugs[1] her. She returns the embrace,[2] somewhat[3] surprised. When he lets go of her, she says: "Now, please don't let Señora Gonzales wait any longer. That's very rude[4]."
Justus rushes outside.

Señora Gonzales is not waiting, but is rummaging through the chests[5] of books in the salvage yard. When she sees Justus coming, she straightens up[6] and smiles. TR. 19
"What wonderful things you have here! And your aunt is a charming lady, she invited[7] me for coffee."
"I have no idea how you managed that," Justus says. "But I'm very grateful[8]."
"Grateful? What for? After all, you're helping us. So will you ask me your questions now?"
"Yes. Although I don't have so many questions anymore. Where is José?"
"Unfortunately, he wouldn't tell us. He's too afraid of Pentecost and his gang[9]."
"Understood[10]. Would you look at a few photos?"
"Of course."
Justus dashes through the fridge door into the half emptied headquarters. He still can hardly believe that his nightmare[11] is over. He

1 to hug: umarmen
2 embrace: Umarmung
3 somewhat: ein wenig, etwas
4 rude: unhöflich
5 chest: Truhe
6 to straighten up: sich aufrichten
7 to invite: einladen
8 grateful: dankbar
9 gang: Bande
10 understood: verstehe
11 nightmare: Alptraum

grabs the photos Bob left on the table and is back with Señora Gonzales in no time.
"Here. Please look through them and tell me if you recognize[1] anyone."
Señora Gonzales looks at the photos.
"Yes … I know that man there."
She holds out the photo to Justus. It shows Pentecost, the man who shot the tyre to pieces[2], as well as a third[3] man who is half hidden by an ice-cream seller.
"Which one?" Justus asks. "The small fat one or the one in the T-shirt?"
"Neither nor[4]. The one next to them. That's the man who came into José's flat shortly before the break-in[5]. His name is Martin Sheffers. He works as a night watchman[6] in the Page Museum."
That is the last piece of the puzzle. "Are you quite sure that he was in José's flat?"
"*Sí*[7]. We know Martin. He visited José often."
"But your husband said that José has no *gringos* as friends."
Señora Gonzales looks at him blankly[8]. "I didn't say that Martin Sheffers is José's friend."
"Then he stole the Madonna?"
"*Sí*. We didn't dare stop him."
"And who wrecked the flat?"
"The clowns did that when they didn't find what they were looking for. And do you know what's strange[9]?"

1 to recognize: wiedererkennen
2 to shoot to pieces: in Stücke zerschießen
3 third: dritte/-r/-s
4 neither nor: weder noch
5 break-in: Einbruch
6 night watchman: Nachtwächter
7 sí *(spanisch)*: ja
8 blankly: ausdruckslos
9 strange: merkwürdig

Justus thought that the tone of her voice[1] was odd[2]. “No, what?” “Martin Sheffers is also one of the clowns,” the woman says. “My husband recognized him.”

Detective Question

Who unexpectedly helps Justus? And who finds the last missing piece of the puzzle that solves the case?

1 voice: Stimme
2 odd: merkwürdig

13. La Brea

TR. 20

A few minutes later, the Andrews family's phone rings[1]. Bob jumps up, but his mother is quicker and grabs the receiver, "Andrews," then in a cold voice, she says, "No, he is not at home. At least not for – Mrs. Jonas?" Bob strains[2] to hear. His mother listens for a while without saying a word. Then she speaks. "Alright, I'll tell him. Bye, Mrs. Jonas." She puts the phone down. "Justus wants you to come to the salvage yard. After everything that has happened, I think you should stay[3] here." She is talking to an empty room. Bob has already left.

Peter is racing[4] around the corner on his bike. Bob nearly runs him over[5]. Justus opens the car door and slips into the back seat. "Get going! Peter, get in quickly!" Peter throws his bike down and jumps into the car. Before he even puts his seat belt[6] on, Bob has already driven off. "Where to?"
"To the museum."
"OK."
Bob accelerates[7]. "Am I right in thinking that everything is OK again?"
"Not only that, but I've solved the puzzle of the Black Madonna."
Justus gives a deep sigh of relief[8] now that they are on their way.
"And you're telling us this, just like that?" Peter says. "What have you found out?"

1 to ring: klingeln
2 to strain: sich anstrengen
3 to stay: bleiben
4 to race: rasen
5 to run sb over: jemanden überfahren
6 seat belt: Sicherheitsgurt
7 to accelerate: Gas geben, beschleunigen
8 sigh of relief: Seufzer der Erleichterung

"Everything," Justus says in a self-satisfied[1] tone. "I know why José's Madonna is black and why Pentecost wants her back at any price, and how the museum thefts are carried out[2]."
"That sounds great," says Bob. "Peter, do you have the article?"
"Yes, here," Peter passes the article to Justus. "Last night, you weren't the only burglar, Justus."

Justus scans[3] the article and nods. "Thought so. And if we're really quick, we might still get hold of the stolen helmet."
"Why? Do you know where it is?"
"Yes."
"And where? Still in the museum? But they searched the whole place!"
"No, not everything." Justus grins. "They overlooked the best hiding place[4]."

Bob avoids the busy streets and approaches the Museum from the north. He drives the VW-Beetle into the parking lot. "No dark green Ford around here." "And no truck[5] either," Peter says.
"No," says Justus, "But this time they can't afford[6] to wait another year to get the loot. Pentecost must know that. Come on!"
Justus doesn't head for the Arts and Crafts Museum or the George C. Page Museum.
"Where are we going?" asks Peter.
"To the pond[7]." Justus points at the glittering, dark surface[8] of the pond in front of them. "Why?" "Because there's something special[9] about the pond."

1 self-satisfied: selbstzufrieden
2 to carry out: begehen
3 to scan: überfliegen
4 hiding place: Versteck
5 truck: LKW
6 to afford: sich leisten
7 pond: Teich
8 glittering, dark surface: glitzernde schwarze Oberfläche
9 special: besonders

"Come and tell us what you found in Pentecost's office!"
"Quite simple," Justus says, "A few chemical formulas."
"Which ones?"
"Monochlorobenzene, trichloroethylene and triethanolamine. Do you know what can be made out of them?"
"Flower pots[1]?" Peter says, sarcastically.
"No, solutions for removing tar[2]. And that over there is not a normal pond. We are in the middle of La Brea – a natural tar pit[3], in which animals have died for thousands of years. The ones that have been exhumed are on display[4] over there in the George C. Page Museum."
"Tar?" Bob repeats, puzzled[5]. "But what has that got to do with the Black Madonna and the golden helmet?"
"Think about it," says Justus. "The Madonna wasn't black when she was on display[6] in the museum. But she was black by the time she ended up in Pentecost's store-room – damaged and worthless[7] for a collector. But not so worthless that he wanted José to have it. And he was busy trying to think of ways of removing the tar."
Peter frowns. "You mean – the Madonna fell into the tar pit when they were in the midst[8] of stealing her? But – "
"Not quite. She was hidden in the tar pit, just like all the other stolen goods. Of course they didn't just throw her into the pit – no diver[9] will jump in after her. So they needed a large but inconspicuous[10] container."
Justus stands still and looks around, searchingly. "Like that?"

1 flower pot: Blumentopf
2 solutions for removing tar: Lösungen, um Teer zu entfernen
3 natural tar pit: natürlich entstandene Teergrube
4 on display: ausgestellt
5 puzzled: verwirrt
6 on display: ausgestellt
7 damaged and worthless: beschädigt und wertlos
8 in the midst of: inmitten, gerade dabei etwas zu tun
9 diver: Taucher
10 inconspicuous: unauffällig

Peter and Bob follow his gaze[1]. "I can only see ..." Bob hesitates. "You don't think that ..." "Yes," says Justus, "That's exactly what I think." The tar pond, glittering and oily, is in front of them. A big and a smaller concrete[2] mammoth stand at the edge[3]. Another mammoth is sunk half into the tar. In a desperate[4] struggle to stay afloat[5], it has pointed its head and trunk up at the sky. The tar is still bubbling[6]. Big bubbles[7] burst[8] on the surface. The air is filled with the smell of burning chemicals. It is a ghostly[9] scene – which becomes even stranger due to the fact that the traffic on nearby Wilshire Boulevard is roaring[10] by. On the other side of the street, skyscrapers tower[11] into the sky, next to 15.000 years of history[12].

A second[13] small mammoth has almost sunk into the tar near the edge of the pit. TR. 21

"Are you crazy?" says Peter. "How can anyone hide anything in there? Thousands of tourists gawp[14] at the pits every day, and they'd immediately see anything buried[15] or hidden in them."

"Neither buried nor hidden. Can't you see that?" Justus points at a small animal that is submerged[16] up to its stomach in the dark, oily water.

1 gaze: starrer Blick
2 concrete: Zement
3 edge: Rand, Kante
4 desperate: verzweifelt
5 afloat: schwimmend
6 bubbling: Blasen werfend
7 bubble: Blase
8 to burst: platzen
9 ghostly: geisterhaft
10 to roar: röhren, brausen
11 skyscrapers tower: Wolkenkratzer türmen
12 history: Geschichte
13 a second: ein/e zweite/r
14 to gawp (*Umgangssprache*): glotzen
15 buried: begraben
16 submerged: versunken

"Wait," says Bob. "That's the small mammoth whose trunk[1] was broken! And which was picked up to be repaired."
"Right," Justus says. "I rang the museum and asked. It was fetched on Sunday. On Tuesday it was already back in its place. And it was fetched by request[2] of the reproduction specialist, Sybil Manning."
"Oh, we're impressed," says Bob. "And what's that got to do with our case?" "You'll see. Come on!" They creep[3] through the shoulder-high reeds[4] growing around the tar pit[5]. Peter steps into a glittering black puddle[6]. He swears[7] as he pulls his foot out. "Justus! Another few steps and we'll drown[8]!"
"Oh, rubbish[9]!" The nearby mammoth looks like a thin elephant. Justus glances at the pond. There is another mammoth on the other side. The Museum of Arts and Crafts is right behind it. "I suppose[10] the thief has put the stolen goods into a waterproof[11] sack and thrown it into that pond over there. And someone else then hauled[12] the sack out with a rope. And then he hid the sack inside the little mammoth until all the excitement[13] was over. The reproduction specialist, Mrs. Manning could easily build[14] a replica[15] which wouldn't have stood out. Help me, Peter." He pulls a rope out of the bag. "We need a lasso."
"Yes, I can do that," Peter says, grinning, and takes the rope from him. "Shall I pull the animal to the shore?"

1 trunk: Rüssel
2 by request: auf Anfrage
3 to creep: kriechen
4 reeds: Schilf
5 tar pit: Teergrube
6 puddle: Pfütze
7 to swear: fluchen
8 to drown: ertrinken
9 rubbish (*Umgangssprache*): Quatsch
10 to suppose: annehmen
11 waterproof: wasserfest
12 to haul: schleppen, befördern
13 excitement: Aufregung
14 to build: bauen
15 replica: Kopie

"Yes, please."
On the second attempt[1], the lasso slips over the mammoth's trunk. Then the Three Investigators pull the rope with all their strength[2]. Justus bends over it, "It should be ... Oh, here it is." There is a click, and suddenly a drawer opens in the replica's tar-stained[3] stomach.
"A secret compartment?" Peter asks. "How did you discover that?"
"It was the only option." Justus says, with satisfaction[4]. "After I realized that the Madonna's black colour was nothing more than tar[5], the rest was simple. There probably was a leak[6] in the packaging[7] in which the Madonna was wrapped[8] and the tar damaged its paint. Do you remember the chemical smell[9] in José's flat? That was tar. José breathed in the poisonous vapours[10] for months and became ill."
"Right," a voice behind Peter says. Something clicks. "Tar is very damaging to the health, as you'll find out in a minute."
Four men come up out of the reeds[11]. They are wearing clown's masks and their frozen grins seem even more horrible than they did on the pier a week ago.
They are holding pistols.
"Take off those silly[12] masks," Justus says, unafraid. "In any case, I think I know who you are. Brian Smith, Martin Sheffers, Steve Bright, and the man for rough stuff[13] who likes shooting holes in tyres.

1 attempt: Versuch
2 strength: Kraft
3 tar-stained: Teer befleckt
4 satisfaction: Befriedigung
5 tar: Teer
6 leak: Leck
7 packaging: Verpackung
8 to wrap: einwickeln, einpacken
9 smell: Geruch
10 poisonous vapours: giftige Ausdünstungen
11 reeds: Schilf
12 silly: albern
13 the man for rough stuff: der Mann für das Grobe

"That's big talk, fatso[1]," says Smith. "Keep that for later – if you are found in 15.000 years. Go and fetch the package out of the animal and give it to me."
Justus hesitates. Peter and Bob look at the street in desperation. This is crazy – only a few steps away, passers-by[2] are walking along without knowing what is happening at the pit. The four men are hidden behind the mammoth's big body. And probably no shots would be heard above the noise of the traffic. "Come on," Smith says and lifts his pistol. "One, two –"
"I will," says Justus, angrily. "But you won't get far. The police will be here in a minute."
"Maybe," says Smith. "But by then it will be too late for you. I warned you not to meddle[3] in our business."
"Why are you even here? You used to wait a year before you fetched the mammoth for repair!"
"We had the nasty feeling[4] that three little snoopers[5] might be nosing[6] around. I've had enough[7] of you now." Smith pulls the trigger[8]. The bullet[9] lands at Justus' feet.
"The next shot will be higher, unless you immediately –"
"Drop your guns[10]!" a voice shouts. "Police! You are surrounded[11]!"
The men freeze[12]. The next moment, Smith grabs Peter, who rams his elbow into Smith's stomach.

1 fatso (*Umgangssprache*): Dickerchen
2 passer-by: Passant
3 to meddle: sich einmischen
4 nasty feeling: böser Verdacht
5 snooper: Schnüffler
6 to nose around: herumstöbern, die Nase hineinstecken
7 enough: genug
8 trigger: Abzug
9 bullet: Geschoss, Projektil
10 gun: Pistole
11 surrounded: umstellt
12 to freeze (*Redewendung*): abrupt stoppen, sich nicht mehr rühren

The man in the blue T-shirt runs through the reeds. Another throws himself under the mammoth and the fourth man grabs Justus. Justus jumps aside. The man trips[1] and falls into the tar with a cry. Justus throws him the end of the rope. The man clings to it. "Help!" he shouts, "Get me out of here!"
Suddenly, there are police everywhere. Smith and the man who was hiding under the mammoth are overpowered[2]. After a short chase[3], the third man is caught. The fourth is pulled out of the tar pit by the policemen. Justus takes an oval package out of the inside of the statue. He unpacks the package carefully and takes out a glittering golden helmet. "There," he says, with satisfaction, "Let's go[4]."

Detective Question

How did a few chemical formulas help Justus to solve the case in the end?

1 to trip: stolpern
2 overpowered: überwältigt
3 chase: Jagd, Verfolgung
4 let's go: lass uns gehen, gehen wir

14. Over and Out[1]

TR. 22

"And where was the Madonna?" Inspector Cotta asks the following[2] Tuesday.
"In Mrs. Manning's shed[3]," Bob answers.
"José had stolen it, but he didn't do anything with it because he was too frightened of Pentecost. Martin Sheffers saw the chance to make money more quickly. After the four thugs[4] threw José into the water, Sheffers broke into José's apartment and took the Madonna. The neighbor Tonio Gonzales saw him. Sheffers intimidated[5] him and disappeared. Later, he came back with the other three clowns – on Pentecost's orders. And, of course, he pretended[6] to be very annoyed[7] that the Madonna had disappeared."
"At home, he then tried to take off the tar," says Peter. "But that probably damaged the paint."
"The museum wants the Madonna back all the same," says Cotta. "I've looked at her – a beautiful piece. I hope she can be restored[8]."
"Have Mr. Pentecost and Sybil Manning already been arrested[9]?" Justus asks.
Cotta nods. "Pentecost was the boss, but Mrs. Manning was the ringleader[10] – she had the idea of planting Sheffers in the George C. Page Museum. Brian Smith organized the museum transports and selected[11] the objects which they would steal. Steve Bright was respon-

1 over and out: Ende der Durchsage
2 following: nächste/r, folgend
3 shed: Schuppen
4 thug: Schlägertyp
5 to intimidate: einschüchtern
6 to pretend: so tun als ob
7 annoyed: verärgert, genervt
8 to restore: restaurieren, wiederherstellen
9 to arrest: verhaften
10 ringleader: Anführer
11 to select: aussuchen

sible[1] for switching off the cameras and lights at the right moment. He was also the one who pretended to be a journalist so he could find out who Peter was."

"The man who did the rough stuff is called Jim Farrell. He stole the objects and handed them to Sheffers. Nobody suspected[2] the employees of the neighboring museum. So Sheffers was able to pack up the loot[3] and hide it in the mammoth without being bothered[4] by anyone. It all worked smoothly[5], until he didn't pack the Madonna statue properly. The tar ruined it. And Pentecost didn't want it for his collection anymore. But he didn't have the heart[6] to destroy[7] it, so he stored it in the loft."

"Where José found her," Peter continues. "He believed she was worthless, but found her beautiful and took her home with him. But then he hid her under his bed for almost seven years. The poisonous tar vapours[8] made him ill, but he thought he was ill because of the curse of the Black Madonna who was punishing[9] him for the theft."

"Pentecost only noticed the theft a few months ago," Bob goes on, "Then the order[10] books were no longer full, and José was dismissed. Soon after that, Pentecost realized that José had taken the Madonna and he threatened[11] him. José grew afraid, but he denied[12] that he had the Madonna. Pentecost didn't believe him and sent the four clowns after him."

1 responsible: verantwortlich
2 to suspect: verdächtigen
3 loot: Beute, Diebesgut
4 to bother: stören
5 it worked smoothly: es ging glatt, es funktionierte reibungslos
6 to have the heart (*Redewendung*): Mut haben, trauen
7 to destroy: zerstören
8 vapour: Ausdünstung
9 to punish: bestrafen
10 order: Bestellung
11 to threaten: drohen
12 to deny: verleugnen, verneinen

"And Martin Sheffers visited José alone. He interrogated[1] José until José told him where the Madonna was," Justus says.
"He had planned to play a double game – to do exactly what José hadn't dared, to blackmail[2] Pentecost. When Smith ran out of patience[3] and threw José off the pier, Sheffers realized that it was getting risky[4]. He left and went to Laguna Street alone. There, he stole the Madonna and hid her. Later, he came back with the other three. But then José suddenly became so ill in the hospital that Sheffers was afraid he would be party to[5] a murder, and he dropped the blackmail[6] plan."
"As we were just talking about José," Cotta says, "you can be grateful to him. He made a statement that he had given you permission to go into his apartment. And as to your break-in at Pentecost's, Justus ..."
"I know," Justus says with a sigh, "I was wrong, and you want me to give back my card." He pulls out his card that reads 'Freelance assistant to the Rocky Beach police' and puts it on the table. "Here you are. I'm sorry."
"So you should be." Cotta takes the card and puts it into his desk drawer. "You read the signs[7] right, but you went too far. I had to listen to a few hostile[8] questions from my Carino Beach colleagues. And you can count yourself lucky[9] that Pentecost's charges have not been upheld[10] as he is in prison himself."
Justus can't believe his ears. "There is no charge?"

1 to interrogate: befragen
2 to blackmail: erpressen
3 to run out of patience (*Redewendung*): die Geduld verlieren
4 risky: riskant
5 to be party to: beteiligt sein, Mittäter sein
6 blackmail: Erpressung
7 sign: Zeichen
8 hostile: ablehnend, feindselig
9 to count oneself lucky (*Redewendung*): sich glücklich schätzen
10 to uphold charges: die Anklage aufrechterhalten

"No. So what shall I do with this card?" Inspector Cotta opens the drawer again, takes out the card and throws it to Justus. "And now get out!"

Detective Question

What was the curse of the Black Madonna? What caused José's illness?

Englisch-Deutsche Wortliste

accelerate – *beschleunigen, Gas geben*
accused – *beschuldigt*
actually – *tatsächlich*
admit – *zugeben*
afford – *sich leisten*
afloat – *schwimmend*
aghast – *entsetzt, entgeistert*
agree – *zustimmen*
aid – *Hilfe*
aim – *zielen*
ajar – *angelehnt, einen Spalt offen*
alarmed – *erschrocken*
annoyed – *verärgert, genervt*
annoying – *ärgerlich*
anonymous – *anonym*
answering machine – *Anrufbeantworter*
apparently – *offensichtlich, anscheinend*
approach – *näher kommen*
approachable – *zugänglich*
approve – *befürworten, bejahen*
area code – *Vorwahl*
argument – *Auseinandersetzung*
arrest – *verhaften*
as well – *auch*
as white as a sheet – *weiß wie ein Laken (Redewendung)*
associate with sb – *mit jemandem verkehren*
assumption – *Vermutung*
assure – *versichern, vergewissern*
astonished – *erstaunt, verblüfft*
at any rate – *jedenfalls, keinesfalls*
at least – *wenigstens, zumindest*
at most – *höchstens*
at once – *sofort*
attempt – *Versuch*
attic – *Dachboden*
authorization – *Ermächtigung*
avoid – *vermeiden*
away – *entfernt*
bad luck – *Pech*
bail – *Kaution*
barbed wire – *Stacheldraht*
barely – *kaum*
base – *Plattform*

be frightened of – *sich fürchten vor*
be grounded – *Hausarrest haben*
be in a fix – *in der Patsche sitzen (Redewendung)*
be party to – *beteiligt sein, Mittäter sein*
be supposed to be for – *bestimmt sein für*
beach – *Strand*
beaded curtain – *Perlenvorhang*
bear – *ertragen*
bed frame – *Bettgestell*
beforehand – *vorher*
beg – *bitten, betteln*
bell – *Klingel*
bench – *Sitzbank*
betray – *verraten, hintergehen*
bite one's lips – *sich auf die Lippen beißen*
blackmail – *1. erpressen, 2. Erpressung*
blade – *Klinge*
blankly – *ausdruckslos*
blaring – *heulend*
Blast! – *Verdammt! Mist! (Umgangssprache)*
blaze – *grell scheinen*
blurred – *verwischt*
booklet – *Broschüre*
bored – *gelangweilt*
bother – *belästigen, stören*
bothered – *gestört*
break – *brechen*
break in – *einbrechen*
break into a flat – *in eine Wohnung einbrechen*
break-in – *Einbruch*
breath – *Atem*
bridge – *Brücke*
brightly colored – *in bunten Farben*
brilliant – *brilliant, genial*
briskly – *energisch, lebhaft*
broad – *breit*
brusquely – *brüsk, barsch*
bubble – *Blase*
bubbling – *Blasen werfend*
build – *bauen*
bullet – *Geschoss, Projektil*
bumpily – *holprig*
burglar – *Einbrecher*
buried – *begraben*
burly – *kräftig, stämmig*
burst – *platzen*
burst out – *herausplatzen*
busy – *beschäftigt*
busy signal – *Besetztzeichen*
by request – *auf Anfrage*

by the way – *übrigens*
cab – *hier: Führerhaus des LKW*
call it a day – *Feierabend machen (Redewendung)*
candle smoke – *Kerzenruß*
carry out – *durchführen, begehen*
carved – *geschnitzt*
cast iron stove – *Ofenherd aus Gusseisen*
catch – *fangen*
catch on – *etwas kapieren*
catch up with sb – *jemanden einholen*
cause – *Grund, Ursache*
ceiling – *Zimmerdecke*
century – *Jahrhundert*
change – *sich umziehen*
change one's mind – *seine Meinung ändern*
chase – *Jagd, Verfolgung*
chest – *1. Brustkorb, 2. Truhe*
chew on sth – *an etwas knabbern, etwas verarbeiten (Redewendung)*
chin – *Kinn*
claim – *behaupten*
climb – *klettern*
clue – *Hinweis, Anhaltspunkt*
coastal town – *Küstenstadt*
coat hooks – *Garderobenhaken*
coincidence – *Zufall*
cold shivers run up and down his spine – *ihm laufen kalte Schauer über den Rücken (Redewendung)*
collapse – *einen Zusammenbruch erleiden*
colleague – *Kollege*
coma – *Koma*
comparison – *Vergleich*
compensation – *Ausgleich, Entschädigung*
compete with – *dagegen ankommen, damit konkurrieren*
complain – *sich beschweren*
concrete – *Zement*
confident – *zuversichtlich*
congratulate – *gratulieren*
connect – *verbinden*
contact lense – *Kontaktlinse*
continuation – *Fortsetzung*
converted – *umgebaut*
convince – *überzeugen*
count oneself lucky – *sich glücklich schätzen (Redewendung)*
counter – *Rezeption, Theke*
cozy – *gemütlich, behaglich*

crane – *recken*
creak – *Knarren*
creep – *schleichen, kriechen*
crew cut – *Bürstenschnitt, Kurzhaarschnitt*
cross paths – *Wege kreuzen*
crouch – *kauern, hocken*
culprit – *Täter, Schuldige/-r*
cupboard – *Schrank*
cure – *Heilung*
curse – *Fluch*
cursed – *verflucht*
curtly – *brüsk, barsch*
cushion – *Kissen*
damage – *Schaden*
damaged – *beschädigt*
dark room – *Dunkelkammer*
dart – *eilen, sausen*
dash – *stürzen*
dealer – *Händler*
deceit – *Betrug*
decide – *entscheiden*
decidedly – *entschieden*
decipher – *entschlüsseln, erkennen*
deed – *Tat*
delete – *löschen*
delivery – *Lieferung*
deny – *leugnen, verneinen*
describe – *beschreiben*
description – *Beschreibung*
deserted – *verlassen*
deserve – *verdienen*
despair – *Verzweiflung*
desperate – *verzweifelt*
despised – *verhasst, verachtenswert*
despite – *trotz(dem)*
destroy – *zerstören*
developer – *Entwickler*
devour – *vertilgen*
dig – *graben*
digit – *Ziffer*
dim – *trüb*
disappear – *verschwinden*
disappointed – *enttäuscht*
discover – *entdecken*
dismantle – *etwas zerlegen, auseinanderbauen*
dismiss – *entlassen, fortschicken*
distance – *Entfernung, Ferne*
distorted – *verzerrt*
distribute – *verteilen*
dive – *tauchen*
diver – *Taucher*
divert – *ablenken*
dizzy – *schwindelig*
donate – *spenden*
donation – *Spende*
donor – *Spender, Förderer*

double up with laughter – *platzen vor Lachen*
doubtfully – *zweifelnd*
drawer – *Schublade*
dreary – *trostlos*
dressed – *angezogen*
drone – *dröhnen*
drop out – *ausfallen*
drown – *ertrinken*
dumbfounded – *verblüfft*
dust – *Staub*
ebony – *Ebenholz*
edge – *Rand, Kante*
effortlessly – *mühelos*
either … or – *entweder … oder*
embrace – *Umarmung*
emerge – *auftauchen, erscheinen*
employee – *Angestellte/r*
employer – *Arbeitgeber*
empty – *1. leer, 2. ausleeren*
engine – *Motor*
engraved – *eingraviert*
enough – *genug*
enter – *hereinkommen*
entrance – *Eingang*
entrepreneur – *Unternehmer*
equally – *gleich, ebenso*
even worse – *sogar noch schlimmer*
evidence – *Beweis, Indiz*
evil – *böse*
excavation site – *Ausgrabungsort*
exchange looks – *Blicke wechseln*
excitement – *Aufregung*
exhaust fumes – *Abgase*
exhausting – *anstrengend*
exhibition – *Ausstellung*
exonerate – *entlasten*
expectation – *Erwartung*
expressionless – *ausdruckslos*
failure – *Ausfall*
fairground – *Jahrmarkt*
fairly – *ziemlich*
fake – *falsch*
fancy – *modisch, protzig*
fatso – *Dickerchen (Umgangssprache)*
fence – *Zaun*
fetch – *holen*
file – *Ordner, Datei*
final evidence – *der letzte noch fehlende Beweis*
find a clue – *einen Hinweis finden*
finger print – *Fingerabdruck*
fire sb – *jemanden kündigen, entlassen*

fixture – *Halterung*
flashlight – *Taschenlampe*
flashy – *auffallend*
flat – *Wohnung*
flee – *flüchten*
flinch – *zucken*
flower pot – *Blumentopf*
follow – *folgen*
followed – *verfolgt*
following – *nächste/r, folgend*
fool – *Narr*
foolproof – *bombensicher*
foot – *Längenmaß, entspricht 30,4 cm*
forcefully – *energisch*
forger – *Fälscher*
former – *ehemalig*
freelancer – *Freischaffender, freier Mitarbeiter*
freeze – *abrupt stoppen, sich nicht mehr rühren (Redewendung)*
freight – *Fracht*
fridge – *Kühlschrank (Abkürzung für refrigerator)*
frown – *die Stirn runzeln*
full of despair – *verzweifelt*
furiously – *wütend*
furnished – *eingerichtet*
furnishing – *Einrichtung*
furniture – *Möbel*
further – *weiter*
furtive – *verstohlen*
gain – *gewinnen, etwas davon haben*
gain entry – *Einlass erlangen*
gang – *Bande*
gap – *Lücke*
garish – *grell*
gasoline – *Benzin*
gate – *Tor*
gaunt – *hager, ausgemergelt*
gawp – *glotzen (Umgangssprache)*
gaze – *(starrer) Blick*
generous – *großzügig*
get rid of sb – *jemanden loswerden*
get stuck in a traffic jam – *im Stau stehen*
ghostly – *geisterhaft*
glance at – *anschauen, einen Blick werfen auf*
gleaming – *strahlend*
glitter – *Glitzer*
glittering – *glänzend*
glitzy – *glitzernd*
gloomy – *düster*
glumly – *mürrisch, betreten*
go astray – *sich auf Abwegen befinden*

go into hiding – *untertauchen (Redewendung)*
goblet – *Kelch*
goddess – *Göttin*
goods – *Waren*
grab – *greifen, grabschen*
grateful – *dankbar*
grave – *Grab*
Great Deliverance – *großartige Lieferung und Erlösung (Wortspiel)*
grim – *düster, grimmig*
grin – *Grinsen*
gringo – *Gringo (Mexikanischer Ausdruck für Weiße/r)*
grit one's teeth – *Zähne knirschen*
grown – *erwachsen*
guide – *Führer*
gun – *Pistole*
guy – *Typ, Kerl (Umgangssprache)*
hair stands on end – *Haare stehen zu Berge (Redewendung)*
hall – *Flur, Korridor*
hastily – *hastig*
haul – *schleppen, befördern*
have the heart – *den Mut haben, sich trauen (Redewendung)*
headed – *mit der Überschrift*
headlight – *Scheinwerfer*
headline – *Überschrift*
headquarters – *Hauptquartier, Zentrale*
headscarf – *Kopftuch*
heap – *Haufen*
heave – *stemmen, hieven*
helmet – *Helm*
hero – *Held*
heroic – *heldenhaft*
hesitate – *zögern*
hidden – *versteckt*
hiding place – *Versteck*
hinge – *Türangel, Scharnier*
hiss – *zischen*
history – *Geschichte*
hoarse – *heiser*
honorary – *ehrenamtlich*
horrified – *entsetzt*
hostile – *feindselig, ablehnend*
however – *jedoch*
hug – *umarmen*
hum – *Summen*
humbly – *demütig*
humming – *Brummen*
hurry – *Eile*
icon – *Ikone*
ID card – *Ausweis*
imprint – *Spur*

imprisoned – *eingesperrt*
in harm's way – *in Gefahr*
in the meantime – *inzwischen*
in the midst of – *inmitten*
in unison – *einstimmig*
include – *einbeziehen*
inconspicuous – *unauffällig, unscheinbar*
incriminate – *belasten*
indeed – *allerdings*
indicator – *Blinker*
injured – *verletzt*
insolence – *Frechheit, Anmaßung*
intently – *aufmerksam*
interrogate – *befragen*
interrupt – *unterbrechen*
interviewee – *Informant*
intimidate – *einschüchtern*
introduce sb – *jemanden vorstellen*
investigation – *Untersuchung*
invite – *einladen*
inviting – *einladend*
involvement – *Beteiligung, Verwicklung*
irritated – *irritiert*
jagged – *gezackt*
judge – *Richter*
junk store – *Schrottwaren-laden*
junk yard – *Schrottplatz (US)*
jurisdiction – *Zuständigkeit, Gerichtsbarkeit*
keyhole – *Schlüsselloch*
lain – *gelegen*
latch – *Türschloss*
lawyer – *Anwalt*
lead – *führen*
leak – *Leck*
leave – *gehen, verlassen, lassen*
Let's go! – *Lass uns gehen! Gehen wir!*
lever – *Hebel*
libel – *Verleumdung*
library – *Bibliothek*
life belt – *Rettungsring*
lifesaving – *Lebensrettung*
line of fire – *Schusslinie*
liquid – *Flüssigkeit*
loading area – *Ladefläche*
locked up – *eingesperrt*
longingly – *sehnsüchtig*
loot – *Beute, Diebesgut*
lose consciousness – *das Bewusstsein verlieren*
luckily – *glücklicherweise*
mad – *verrückt*
make a run for it – *abhauen (Redewendung)*

make onself comfortable – *es sich bequem/gemütlich machen*
mammoth – *Mammut*
manage – *schaffen*
managed – *geschafft*
manufacture – *herstellen*
marble – *Marmor*
matters – *Angelegenheiten*
meddle – *sich einmischen*
melt – *schmelzen*
mention – *erwähnen*
mess – *Durcheinander*
metal rod – *Eisenstange*
MG – *Britische Automarke*
miracle – *Wunder*
missing – *fehlend, vermisst*
mistake – *Fehler*
mistrust – *misstrauen*
murmur – *murmeln*
Museum of Arts & Crafts – *Museum für Kunsthandwerk*
mutter – *murmeln*
narrow – *schmal*
nasty – *gemein*
nasty feeling – *böser Verdacht*
natural tar pit – *natürlich entstandene Teergrube*
nearly – *beinahe*
neglected – *schäbig, vernachlässigt*
neighboring – *benachbart*
neither ... nor – *weder ... noch*
nephew – *Neffe*
newspaper clipping – *Zeitungsausschnitt*
night watchman – *Nachtwächter*
nightmare – *Alptraum*
nod – *nicken*
north – *nördlich*
nose around – *herumstöbern, die Nase hineinstecken*
not even slightly – *nicht im geringsten, kein bisschen*
note – *Notiz*
notice – *bemerken*
numb – *gefühllos, taub*
number plate – *Nummernschild*
oak – *Eiche*
obliging – *entgegenkommend*
obviously – *offensichtlich*
odd – *seltsam, eigenartig*
off guard – *unachtsam, überrumpelt*
on display – *ausgestellt*

onlooker – *Zuschauer, Schaulustiger*
opportunity – *Gelegenheit*
order – *1. Bestellung, 2. befehlen*
ordinary – *gewöhnlich, normal*
over and out – *Ende der Durchsage*
overpowered – *überwältigt*
overtake – *überholen*
overturned – *umgestürzt*
overweight – *übergewichtig*
packaging – *Verpackung*
padlock – *Vorhängeschloss*
pain – *Schmerz*
pale – *blass*
paralyzed – *gelähmt*
parking lot – *Parkplatz*
part – *Teil*
pass out – *bewusstlos werden*
passenger – *Beifahrer*
passer-by – *Passant*
patience – *Geduld*
peace – *Frieden*
peep – *(verstohlen) schauen*
peer – *spähen, forschend blicken*
perhaps – *vielleicht*
periscope – *Periskop*
permission – *Genehmigung*
pierce – *stechen, blenden*
piled – *gestapelt*
pilgrimage – *Pilgerreise*
pillar – *Pfeiler*
pleasure – *Genuss, große Freude*
poisoned – *vergiftet*
poisonous – *giftig*
poke one's nose in – *sich einmischen, seine Nase hineinstecken*
pond – *Teich*
power cut – *Stromausfall*
praise – *loben*
pray – *beten*
pretend – *so tun als ob*
prevent – *verhindern*
previous – *vorherig*
print out – *Ausdruck*
promise – *versprechen*
promoter – *Förderer*
proof – *Beweis/e*
property – *Gelände, Besitz*
public – *Öffentlichkeit*
publisher – *Herausgeber*
puddle – *Pfütze*
punch – *boxen*
punish – *bestrafen*
puppet – *Handpuppe, Marionette*
puzzled – *verwirrt*

quarrel – *streiten, sich anlegen mit*
race – *rasen*
ragged – *zerfetzt*
ransacked – *durchwühlt, geplündert*
rascal – *Bengel, Gauner*
razor-toothed tiger – *Säbelzahntiger*
reach – *erreichen*
realize – *begreifen*
reason – *Grund*
receiver – *Hörer*
recess – *Nische*
recognize – *wiedererkennen*
record – *Akte*
recording – *Aufnahme*
recover – *sich erholen*
red-breasted flycatcher – *Rotbauchfliegenschnäpper (Vogelname)*
reeds – *Schilf*
refuse – *verweigern*
regret – *bereuen*
release – *Entlassung*
reluctantly – *widerstrebend*
remain silent – *stillbleiben*
remains – *Überreste*
remove – *entfernen*
replica – *Kopie*
reproduction – *Nachbildung*
required – *notwendig, erforderlich*
rescue – *retten*
research – *Forschung*
resist – *Widerstand leisten, widerstreben*
responsible – *verantwortlich*
restore – *restaurieren, wiederherstellen*
rethink – *überdenken*
return – *zurückkehren*
revenge – *Rache*
reward – *Belohnung*
ring – *klingeln*
ringleader – *Anführer*
risky – *riskant*
roar – *röhren, brausen*
roaring – *rauschend*
rob – *ausrauben*
rough stuff – *das Grobe (Umgangssprache)*
roughly – *rau*
row – *Reihe*
Rubbish! – *Quatsch! (Umgangssprache)*
rude – *unhöflich*
rummage about – *herumstöbern, wühlen*
run out of patience – *die Geduld verlieren (Redewendung)*

run sb over – *jemanden überfahren*
rusty – *rostig*
safety – *Sicherheit*
sag – *herabsinken*
salvage yard – *Schrottplatz*
satisfaction – *Befriedigung*
sauce – *Soße*
scan – *überfliegen*
scorching heat – *sengende Hitze*
scrap yard – *Schrottplatz* (UK)
screeching – *quietschend*
scrutinize – *inspizieren, kritisch blicken, mustern*
search – *durchsuchen*
search warrant – *Durchsuchungsbefehl*
seat belt – *Sicherheitsgurt*
second – *zweite/-r/-s*
secret compartment – *Geheimfach*
seldom – *selten*
select – *aussuchen*
selflessly – *selbstlos*
self-satisfied – *selbstzufrieden*
serve – *dienen*
set – *untergehen (Sonne)*
settle down – *sich niederlassen*
severe – *ernst*
shabby street – *heruntergekommene Straße*
shades of skin – *(Schattierungen der) Hautfarben*
shadow – *Schatten*
shadowy – *schattenhaft*
shake – *schütteln*
shark – *Hai*
shed – *Schuppen*
shelf – *Regal*
shoe cupboard – *Schuhschrank*
shoot to bits/pieces – *in Stücke zerschießen*
shore – *Küste*
showcase – *Schaukasten, Vitrine*
shrink back – *zurückschrecken, ausweichen*
shrug one's shoulders – *mit den Schultern zucken*
shudder – *zittern, stottern*
shutters – *Fensterläden*
sí – *ja (spanisch)*
sigh – *seufzen*
sigh of relief – *Seufzer der Erleichterung*
sign – *Zeichen*

silent – *still*
silly – *albern*
siren – *Sirene*
skeleton key – *Dietrich, Multifunktionsschlüssel*
skyscraper – *Wolkenkratzer*
slam sth shut – *etwas zuschlagen*
slander – *verleumden*
slimy – *schmierig*
slippers – *Pantoffeln, Hausschuhe*
slit open – *aufgeschlitzt*
small-time artist – *Kleinkünstler*
small-time thief – *kleiner Dieb*
smashing – *grandios (Umgangssprache)*
smeared – *beschmiert*
smell – *Geruch*
smoothly – *glatt, reibungslos*
sniff – *schnuppern*
snoop – *schnüffeln*
snooper – *Schnüffler*
so far – *bisher*
soaked – *durchnässt*
soaked in sweat – *schweißüberströmt*
soft drinks – *Erfrischungsgetränke*
solution – *Lösung*
solve the case – *den Fall lösen*
somewhat – *ein wenig, etwas*
spare tyre – *Reserverad*
special – *besonders*
speechless – *sprachlos*
spend – *verbringen*
spin – *wirbeln*
splash – *Platscher, Aufspritzen*
splinter – *Splitter, Spreißel, Holzspan*
spoil – *verderben*
spread – *ausbreiten*
spread like bushfire – *sich verbreiten wie ein Lauffeuer (Redewendung)*
spread out – *ausbreiten*
squeak – *quietschen, kreischen*
squeeze – *quetschen*
stacked – *gestapelt*
stare – *starrer Blick*
stare into space – *ins Leere starren*
staring – *Starren*
statement – *(Zeugen)aussage*
stay – *bleiben*

stealthily – *verstohlen*
steer – *steuern, lenken*
stick out – *herausragen*
sticky – *klebrig*
stomach – *Bauch, Magen*
stop dead – *erstarren*
stove pipe – *Ofenrohr*
straighten up – *sich aufrichten*
strain – *sich anstrengen*
strange – *merkwürdig*
strength – *Kraft*
stretch – *sich strecken, dehnen*
stretcher – *Trage, Tragbahre*
stroll – *spazieren, flanieren*
struggle – *ringen, dagegen ankämpfen*
stumble – *stolpern*
stutter – *stottern*
submerged – *versunken*
suggestion – *Vorschlag*
Sunday edition – *Sonntagsausgabe*
superstition – *Aberglaube*
superstitious – *abergläubisch*
support – *Unterstützung*
suppose – *annehmen*
surface – *Oberfläche*
surprisingly – *überraschend*
surrounded – *umstellt*
surveillance and lighting system – *Überwachungs- und Beleuchtungssystem*
suspect – *verdächtigen*
suspicion – *Verdacht*
suspicious – *verdächtig*
swallow – *schlucken*
sway – *schwanken*
swear – *fluchen*
swiftly – *schnell*
swing shut – *zufallen, zuschwingen*
take a deep breath – *tief Luft holen*
take possession – *in Besitz nehmen*
tanned – *braungebrannt*
tar – *Teer*
tar pit – *Teergrube*
tar-stained – *mit Teer befleckt*
tear open – *aufreißen*
tease – *hänseln, necken*
temptation – *Versuchung*
tense – *angespannt*
theft – *Diebstahl*
thin – *dünn*
third – *dritte/-r/-s*
threat – *Drohung*
threaten – *bedrohen*
threatening – *drohend*

throat – *Kehle, Hals*
throw sb a glance – *jemandem einen Blick zuwerfen*
thug – *Schlägertyp*
tide – *Flut*
tinker – *basteln, ausprobieren*
tiptoe – *schleichen, auf Zehenspitzen gehen*
topple over – *umfallen*
toss – *werfen, schleudern*
touch – *berühren*
tough – *rau, zäh*
tow away – *abschleppen*
tower – *sich türmen*
trace – *Spur*
tradesman – *Händler*
trailer – *Wohnwagen, Campinganhänger*
trap – *Falle*
tray – *Tablett*
treasure map – *Schatzkarte*
treat – *behandeln*
tremble – *zittern*
trembling – *zitternd*
trigger – *Abzug*
trip – *stolpern*
trouble – *Ärger, Probleme, Schwierigkeiten*
troublesome – *lästig, störend*
truck – *LKW*
trunk – *Rüssel*
turn up – *auftauchen (Umgangssprache)*
tyre – *Reifen*
unappetizing – *unappetitlich*
unawares – *überrascht, unaufmerksam*
unfortunate – *unglücklich, ungünstig*
unfortunately – *leider*
unimpressed – *unbeeindruckt*
unpleasant – *unerfreulich*
untie – *losbinden*
unwilling – *unwillig, unkooperativ*
uphold charges – *die Anklage aufrechterhalten*
upper stories – *obere Stockwerke*
urgently – *dringend*
useful – *nützlich*
usual – *gewöhnlich, üblicherweise*
valuable – *wertvoll*
vapour – *Dampf, Ausdünstung*
victim – *Opfer*
violently – *heftig*
visibly – *sichtbar*
visitor – *Besucher*

voice – *Stimme*
voicemail – *Anrufbeantworter auf Mailbox*
wail – *heulen*
wailing – *Geheul*
waterproof – *wasserfest*
wave – *Welle*
wealthy – *wohlhabend, reich*
weight – *Gewicht*
what with – *wegen (Redewendung)*
Where the heck ...? – *Wo zum Teufel...? (Umgangssprache)*
wince – *zusammenzucken*
winding – *kurvenreich, kurvig*
with drawn pistols – *mit gezückten Pistolen*
with emphasis – *mit Nachdruck, betont*
witness – *Zeuge*
work – *funktionieren*
working space – *Arbeitsplatz*
workshop – *Werkstatt*
worship – *Anbetung, Verehrung*
worth – *wert*
worthless – *wertlos*
wrap – *einwickeln, einpacken*
wreck – *demolieren, zerstören*
yard – *Längenmaß, entspricht 91,44 cm*
yell – *rufen, schreien*
You are attached to your stuff. – *Du hängst an deinem Zeug. (Umgangssprache)*
zoom off – *davonbrausen*

Nützliche Detektiv-Ausdrücke

Hier sind einige Vokabeln und Redewendungen, die hilfreich sind, wenn man über Verbrechen und Detektivarbeit spricht.

arrest someone – *jemanden festnehmen*
be sent to prison – *ins Gefängnis gesteckt werden*
break into a house – *in ein Haus einbrechen*
case – *Fall*
catch up with someone – *jemanden einholen*
collect evidence – *Beweismaterial/Hinweise sammeln*
commit a crime – *ein Verbrechen begehen*
commit sabotage – *Sabotage begehen*
criminal – *Krimineller, Verbrecher*
detective – *Detektiv*
discover a clue – *einen Hinweis entdecken*
drop one's weapon – *seine Waffe fallen lassen*
evidence – *Beweismaterial*
figure something out – *etwas herausfinden*
Freeze! – *Keine Bewegung!*
guilty – *schuldig*
innocent – *unschuldig*
investigate a case – *in einem Fall ermitteln*
investigation – *Ermittlung*
investigator – *ein Ermittler, eine Ermittlerin*
launch an investigation – *eine Ermittlung starten*
look out for something – *auf etwas achten*
point a gun/pistol at someone – *ein Gewehr/eine Pistole auf jemanden richten*
prove that someone is guilty/innocent – *beweisen, dass jemand schuldig/unschuldig ist*
pursue someone – *jemanden verfolgen*
robbery – *ein Raubüberfall, ein Diebstahl*

Übungen

1 Word Chain

Böse Schlange oder nette Schlange? Finde alle Adjektive, die in den beiden Wortschlangen versteckt sind. Aber Vorsicht, lass dich von der bösen Schlange nicht beißen!

Tipp!
Adjektive helfen dabei, eine Sache oder Person zu beschreiben.

2 Wortschatz

Hier sind einige Substantive verlorengegangen! Sie haben sich gut versteckt! Kannst du mit Hilfe der Beschreibungen die fehlenden Wörter herausfinden?

1. It's something that you make, but you are not happy when you made one. Teachers correct it.

   It's a m _ _ _ _ _ _ .

2. An investigator wants to find a criminal. Before he finds the right person, he first of all gathers information about the crime.

   Then he has a s _ _ _ _ _ _ _ _ .

3. Witches can do it. People are afraid of it. The Black Madonna had it.

   It's a c _ _ _ _ .

4. He likes expensive things. He comes at night. He doesn't use a normal key. Who is it?

   It's a b _ _ _ _ _ _ .

5. Kids love it. Teachers hate it. The Three Investigators can't relax during it. In summer it's six weeks long.

   It's a h _ _ _ _ _ _ .

3 Crossword Puzzle

Was muss ein guter Detektiv können und erkennen? Ergänze das Kreuzworträtsel mit den passenden englischen Übersetzungen der deutschen Begriffe. Findest du auch das Lösungswort?

Waagerecht

1. Antwort: *answer*
2. verhindern
3. schreiben
4. nachfragen
5. Auto
6. Fehler

Senkrecht

7. Fall
8. Lösung: *solution*
9. Füller, Kuli
10. rennen
11. lösen
12. Suche
13. anführen, leiten

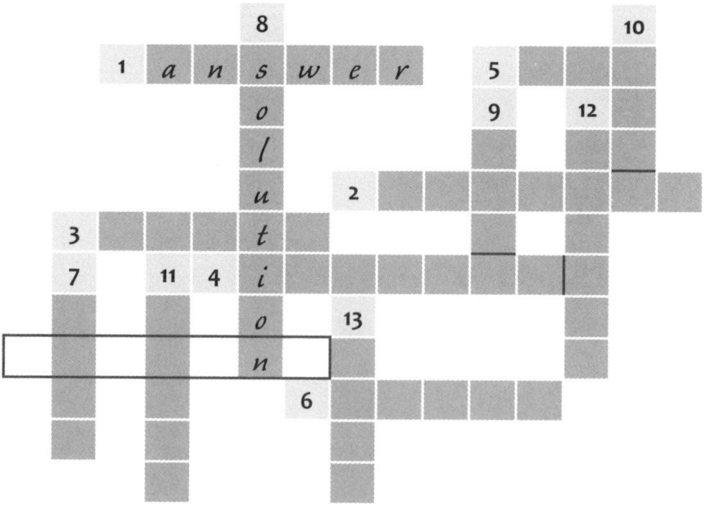

Lösungswort: M _ _ _ _ _ _ _

4 Im Museum

Bist du auch ein Kunstsammler? Umkreise alle Wörter, die etwas mit Kunst zu tun haben und streiche die unpassenden Vokabeln durch.

> pier, colored, investigation, goblet,
> burglary, reproduction, shark, showcase,
> chap, painting, reporter, poison

5 Zusammengesetzte Wörter

Tipp!
Zwei Substantive können zusammen ein neues Wort ergeben! Das nennt man dann **compound.** Aber aufgepasst: Manche **compounds** werden getrennt und manche zusammen geschrieben!

Oje, hier hat jemand das Fenster offen gelassen, und ein starker Luftzug hat alle Wörter durcheinandergewirbelt. Welche beiden Wörter ergeben jeweils zusammen ein neues Wort? Verbinde die acht Wortpaare, die zusammengehören und schreibe sie auf. Findest du auch das neunte zusammengesetzte Substantiv, das sich hier versteckt hat?

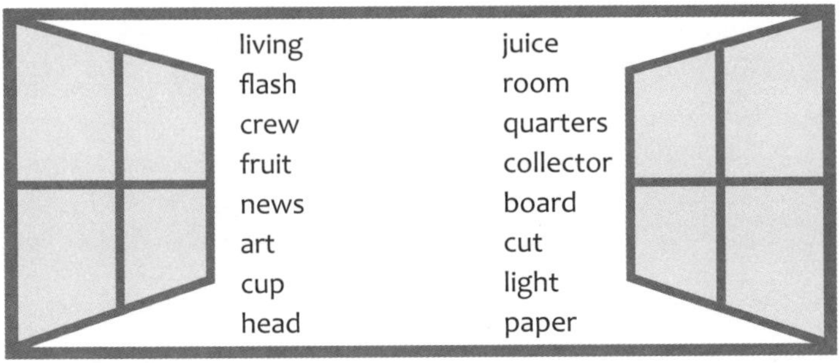

living	juice
flash	room
crew	quarters
fruit	collector
news	board
art	cut
cup	light
head	paper

1. *living room – Wohnzimmer*
2. ______________________
3. ______________________
4. ______________________
5. ______________________
6. ______________________
7. ______________________
8. ______________________
9. Hier ist das versteckte Substantiv: **h** _ _ _ _ _ _ _ _ _

6 Adjektiv oder Adverb?

Hier ist Justus die Schere ausgerutscht! Schnell, her mit dem Kleber! Was sagst du als Meisterdetektiv dazu? Kannst du die Schnipsel wieder zusammenfügen, wo es notwendig ist? Brauchst du jeweils ein Adjektiv oder ein Adverb? Verbinde oder streiche die Endung **-ly** durch.

Hier noch ein Trick aus der Trickkiste: Eines der Adjektive wird durch die Endung **-ly** nicht zum dazu passenden Adverb. Finde und umkreise das Wort und schreibe es dann in die Trickkiste.

Tipp!
Adverbien beschreiben ein Verb, also eine Tätigkeit oder Aktion näher. Sie haben häufig die Endung **-ly**.

1. The multinational ly city Los Angeles is represented by all shades of skin, ages and all classes.
2. Peter longing ly looks at the huge waves which are crashing on the beach shore.
3. The man stares cold ly at Justus; then he turns around without a word and walks on.
4. He opens his eyes and looks around in the dim ly water.
5. The gaunt ly face has assumed a severe ly hard ly expression.
6. Aunt Mathilda answers reluctant ly , "Thank you. Come in, Justus."

Trickkiste	
h _ _ _	**h** _ _ _ _ _ _
hart	*kaum*
Mit der Endung **-ly** ändert sich die Bedeutung des Wortes!	

7 British English und American English

Wusstest du schon, dass es im Britischen und Amerikanischen Englisch unterschiedliche Wörter gibt, die aber dieselbe Bedeutung haben? Verbinde jeweils die beiden Ausdrücke, die dasselbe bedeuten und ergänze anschließend die deutsche Übersetzung.

Tipp! Manchmal unterscheiden sich die Wörter auch nur durch die Schreibweise!

British English	American English	German

lorry	junk yard	S _ _ _ _ _ _ _ _ _ _ _
tyre	vacation	U _ _ _ _ _
coloured	garbage can	M _ _ _ _ _ _ _ _
chap	truck	L _ _
holiday	**colored**	**farbig**
parking place	neighbor	N _ _ _ _ _ _
scrap yard	guy	K _ _ _
rubbish bin	parking lot	P _ _ _ _ _ _ _ _
neighbour	tire	R _ _ _ _ _

8 Good guy or bad guy?

Justus braucht deine Hilfe! Wem sollen die Handschellen verpasst werden? Findest du alle sieben Bösewichte? Markiere alle Bezeichnungen für böse oder kriminelle Mitmenschen.

chap	clown	burglar	tradesman
peer	hero	onlooker	robber
colleague	lawyer	reporter	rascal
investigator	neighbor	aunt	thug
pilgrim	culprit	owner	lad
employer	thief	collector	forger

9 Wem gehört was?

Hier hat ein Einbrecher gewütet und alles durcheinander gebracht. Inspektor Cotta ist verzweifelt! Kannst du alles wieder richtig zuordnen? Ergänze die folgenden Sätze mit den jeweils passenden Possessivbegleitern.

your, his, our, his, his, their, my, her

1. Justus has an uncle. Uncle Titus is ______________ uncle.
2. The forger has a statue. It's not ______________ statue.
3. Peter's mother is nice. He is ______________ son.
4. The Three Investigators don't have a car. This Rolls Royce isn't ______________ car.
5. You are a rascal! Inspector Cotta knows ______________ name.
6. I have a secretary. ______________ desk is bigger than her desk.

7. The trader sells many goods. ______________ pockets are full of money.
8. We love to read crime stories. ______________ books are great.

10 Back to the Present

Die drei ??? sind in ein Zeitloch gefallen! Wer hilft ihnen wieder heraus? Ergänze die folgenden Sätze mit der jeweils richtigen Zeitform der Verben in Klammern. Achte darauf, ob etwas gerade im Moment stattfindet **(Present Progressive)** oder ob es sich um eine allgemeingültige Aussage **(Simple Present)** handelt.

1. The collector ________________ *(to love)* paintings.
2. Justus ________________ *(to walk)* on the beach.
3. The clown ________________ *(to wear)* a mask.
4. The city ________________ *(to be)* very large.
5. The Mexican ________________ *(to speak)* quickly.
6. The waves ________________ *(to crash)* against the pier.
7. The car ________________ *(to look)* very expensive.
8. The thief ________________ *(to steal)* diamonds.
9. The robber ________________ *(to have)* many keys.
10. The publisher ________________ *(to like)* good books.
11. The Three Investigators ________________ *(to solve)* a lot of cases.
12. Uncle Titus ________________ *(to own)* a scrap yard.

11 Geklaut!

Oh, ein Dieb hat sämtliche Bindestriche entwendet! Kannst du Justus helfen und an der jeweils richtigen Stelle die fehlenden Bindestriche einsetzen? Der Dieb hat Justus auch noch eine Falle gestellt, denn eine der Zahlen wird als ein Wort geschrieben.

Tipp!
Wusstest du schon, dass *eine Milliarde* auf Englisch **a billion** heißt? Und übrigens, den *Bindestrich* nennt man im Englischen **hyphen**!

1. two thousand
2. twenty three
3. four million
4. fifty seven
5. six teen
6. forty eight
7. six hundred
8. three billion

Lösungen

Detective Questions

Hast du die Antworten gefunden? Die Detektivfragen sollen zum Nachdenken anregen. Hier gibt es keine Bewertung, kein richtig oder falsch. Dein Spürsinn ist hier gefragt!

1 Word Chain

Schlange 1
violent: *heftig*
pale: *blass*
soaked: *durchnässt*
empty: *leer*
fake: *gefälscht*

Schlange 2
confident: *zuversichtlich*
effortless: *mühelos*
equal: *gleichwertig*
easy: *leicht*

2 Wortschatz

1. It's something that you make, but you are not happy when you made one. Teachers correct it.

   It's a **mistake**.

2. An investigator wants to find a criminal. Before he finds the right person, he first of all gathers information about the crime.

   Then he has a **suspicion**.

3. Witches can do it. People are afraid of it. The Black Madonna had it.

   It's a **curse**.

4. He likes expensive things. He comes at night. He doesn't use a normal key. Who is it?

   It's a **burglar**.

5. Kids love it. Teachers hate it. The Three Investigators can't relax during it. In summer it's six weeks long.

   It's a **holiday**.

3 Crossword Puzzle

Waagerecht

1. Antwort: **answer**
2. verhindern: **prevent**
3. schreiben: **write**
4. nachfragen: **inquire**
5. Auto: **car**
6. Fehler: **error**

Senkrecht

7. Fall: **case**
8. Lösung: **solution**
9. Füller, Kuli: **pen**
10. rennen: **run**
11. lösen: **solve**
12. Suche: **search**
13. anführen, leiten: **lead**

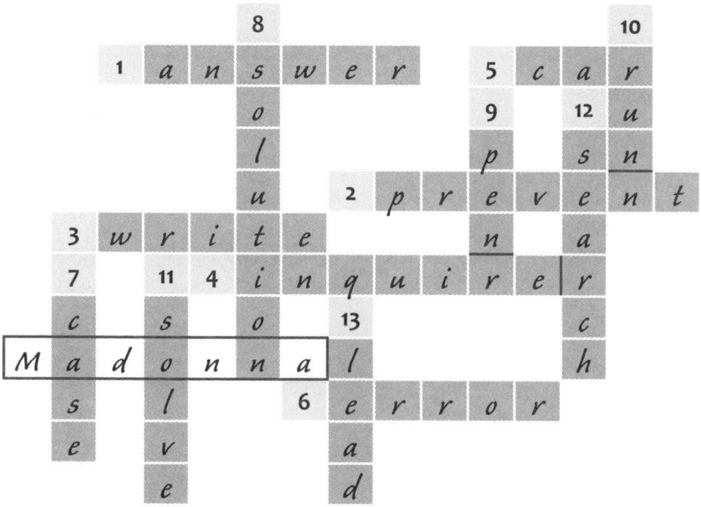

Lösungswort: **Madonna**

4 Im Museum

Die folgenden Wörter haben etwas mit Kunst zu tun:

colored: *farbig*
goblet: *Kelch*
reproduction: *Reproduktion, Kopie des Originals*
showcase: *Vitrine*
painting: *Gemälde*

5 Zusammengesetzte Wörter

1. living room: *Wohnzimmer*
2. flashlight: *Taschenlampe*
3. crew cut: *Bürstenhaarschnitt*
4. fruit juice: *Obstsaft*
5. newspaper: *Zeitung*
6. art collector: *Kunstsammler*
7. cupboard: *Geschirrschrank, Küchenschrank*
8. headquarters: *Hauptquartier*
9. headlight: *Autoscheinwerfer*

6 Adjektiv oder Adverb?

1. *Adjektiv*
   The multinational city Los Angeles is represented by all shades of skin, ages and all classes.

2. *Adverb*
   Peter longingly looks at the huge waves which are crashing on the beach shore.

3. *Adverb*
   The man stares coldly at Justus; then he turns around without a word and walks on.

4. *Adjektiv*
   He opens his eyes and looks around in the dim water.

5. *Adjektive* und *Adverb*
   The gaunt face has assumed a severely hard expression.

6. *Adverb*
   Aunt Mathilda answers reluctantly, "Thank you. Come in, Justus."

Trickkiste	
hard	**hardly**
hart	*kaum*

Mit der Endung **-ly** ändert sich die Bedeutung des Wortes!

7 British English und American English

British English	American English	German

lorry	junk yard	*Schrottplatz*
tyre	vacation	*Urlaub*
coloured	garbage can	*Mülleimer*
chap	truck	*LKW*
holiday	colored	*farbig*
parking place	neighbor	*Nachbar*
scrap yard	guy	*Kerl (Typ)*
rubbish bin	parking lot	*Parkplatz*
neighbour	tire	*Reifen*

8 Good guy or bad guy?

Das hier sind die Bösewichte:

burglar: *Einbrecher*
robber: *Räuber*
rascal: *Bengel, Gauner*
thug: *Schläger(typ)*
culprit: *Übeltäter*
thief: *Dieb*
forger: *Fälscher*

9 Wem gehört was?

1. Justus has an uncle. Uncle Titus is **his** uncle.
2. The forger has a statue. It's not **his** statue.
3. Peter's mother is nice. He is **her** son.
4. The Three Investigators don't have a car. This Rolls Royce isn't **their** car.
5. You are a rascal! Inspector Cotta knows **your** name.
6. I have a secretary. **My** desk is bigger than her desk.
7. The trader sells many goods. **His** pockets are full of money.
8. We love to read crime stories. **Our** books are great.

10 Back to the Present

1. The collector **loves** paintings.
2. Justus **is walking** on the beach.
3. The clown **is wearing** a mask.
4. The city **is** very large.
5. The Mexican **is speaking** quickly.
6. The waves **are crashing** against the pier.
7. The car **looks** very expensive.
8. The thief **is stealing** diamonds.
9. The robber **has** many keys.

10. The publisher **likes** good books.
11. The Three Investigators **solve** a lot of cases.
12. Uncle Titus **owns** a scrap yard.

11 Geklaut!

1. two thousand
2. twenty-three
3. four million
4. fifty-seven
5. **sixteen**
6. forty-eight
7. six hundred
8. three billion